The Divine Right of Capital

BOOKS BY C. E. AYRES

The Theory of Economic Progress

The Divine Right of Capital

The
DIVINE RIGHT
of
CAPITAL

C. E. AYRES

HOUGHTON MIFFLIN COMPANY · BOSTON

1946

The Riverside Press Cambridge

The Riverside Press
CAMBRIDGE · MASSACHUSETTS
PRINTED IN THE U.S.A.

... A<small>MONG</small> the business and professional classes and their economic supporters the conviction holds that any property or income legally acquired represents the productive services rendered by its recipient, either in the way of skilled brain or hand work, thrift, risks, or enterprise, or as inheritance from one who has thus earned it. The notion that any such property or income can contain any payment which is excessive, or the product of superior bargaining power, never enters their minds. Writers to *The Times*, protesting against a rise in the Income Tax, always speak of their 'right' to the income they have 'made,' and regard any tax as a grudging concession to the needs of an outsider, the State.

So long as this belief prevails all serious attempts by a democracy to set the production and distribution of income upon an equitable footing will continue to be met by the organized resistance of the owning classes, which, if they lose control of the political machinery, will not hesitate to turn to other methods of protecting their 'rights.' — J. A. Hobson, *Confessions of an Economic Heretic*.

Contents

Part i. ABSOLUTE CAPITALISM

Part ii. THE FLOW OF INCOME

PART III.   LIMITED CAPITALISM

Part I

ABSOLUTE CAPITALISM

1

Capitalism

CAPITALISM, as the name faintly suggests, is a society in which capital plays the title rôle. There has been only one; our own, and that is rapidly changing into something else. What is chiefly evident at present is confusion. No one can say how long this confusion will last nor how severe it may become. It may even prove fatal. But we can say with certainty that, if it does not actually prove fatal, it will last only until the world grasps the idea of abundance, the possibility of which already exists in large-scale industrial mass production. When this idea has once been grasped, the reality will be achieved forthwith.

Capital also is an idea, not a thing. It is the idea to which we owe the scarcity from which depressions, wars, and revolutions germinate. This idea can be stated very simply, though it will not at first be clearly visible to people who have been cross-eyed all their lives. It is the idea that two quite different things are one and the same thing.

In order to see these two different things as one, you have to be cross-eyed. This is a difficult feat, especially for a whole people. But we have managed it, partly with the help of the economists and partly by force of circumstances.

Economists are members of a highly skilled profession. By long practice and by use of a multitude of adroit literary devices they have been able to bring the art of double-vision and double-talk to a high degree of perfection. An eminent professor of law once defined the legal mind in this way. If, he said, there are two things so closely related that one cannot be conceived except in terms of the other, but if you do think of one without thinking of the other, then you have a legal mind. In somewhat similar fashion it might be said that if two things are utterly and completely distinct, but if you nevertheless think of them as being identical, then you have an economic mind.

But we must not give the professional thinkers too much credit. Economists have done only what professional thinkers always do: they have organized and systematized the ideas of the community. If the basic ideas are right, the system will be right; if they are wrong, the system will be wrong. A community that has learned to use spectacles and so has correct ideas of the basic principle of magnification has thereby laid the foundation for a whole system of scientific knowledge based on magnification by telescope and microscope. But a community that has false ideas of its own superiority to other communities thereby lays the foundation for a whole system of nonsense such as Nazi ideologists have concocted doubtless with complete sincerity and with quite amazing ingenuity.

The circumstances which have directed our economic thinking throughout modern times will be obvious to everybody as soon as history has given us a little perspective on our past. Recent changes have already given us some perspective. That is why we can already begin to see what has happened to us.

Ours is a commercial society. Commerce, purchase and sale, the exchange of goods in the market: these activities have played so large a part in modern life that they have for a time seemed to be the whole thing. In the words of President Coolidge, the business of America is business — buying and selling, making money.

In our society money is power. Money makes the mare go. When any one of us allows himself to daydream, what does he imagine? How do we symbolize success and happiness? Everybody knows! We dream of being rich.

Why do we do this? It is no answer to say that money does confer power on its owner, that most of us would indeed be better off if we had more of it. Why should this be? Why does society recognize this symbol? Why do we honor money-claims which in many cases we all recognize to be quite preposterous? Again, it is no answer to say that we are bound by law to recognize legally valid claims. On what basic idea does such a legal system rest?

To all such questions there can be but one answer. Our whole society is profoundly convinced that money is good in and of itself; that it is good for society no less than for individuals; indeed, that the progress of society itself depends upon the accumulation of money.

This is the idea of capital. Unfortunately for all of us, it is quite false. As everybody knows, the progress of any society depends upon its ability to enlarge the productive apparatus of the community. The recent war has given us a very clear and conspicuous illustration of this process. But since money will buy anything in a commercial society, those who control accumulations of money are in a position to buy and control the increasing productive apparatus that spells progress. Therefore, it *seems* that money *is* the instrument of progress.

That is what we mean by 'capital.' Capital is the money that capitalists accumulate. Capital is also the physical plant of industry that engineers design and workmen build with materials that other workmen fabricate with previously designed and built machines. These two, it seems, are one. Both are capital — and blessed be capital, for without it no economic progress is possible!

This is a very potent idea. Our society has been dominated by it more than by any other for something like four centuries. That is why it has come to be known as capitalism.

2

How It Happened

Societies make mistakes. They also make discoveries. The
discoveries mean progress. But the discoveries get mixed
up with the mistakes, and this retards the progress. That is
what happened in the case of capitalism.

In our society money is power. This power derives from
the institution of property which we have inherited from
feudalism. In the feudal order control of property, especially property in land and in the means of working the land,
was tied up with hereditary rank. But these two principles,
of property and rank, were never absolutely inseparable.
Even in feudal times some things were bought and sold, and
some forms of property were disposable more or less regardless of rank.

What happened then was that feudal rank began to
dwindle in importance while the importance of property increased. This change was of course hard for the feudal aristocracy to bear. The blue bloods fought it as hard as they
could and the Church denounced it bitterly. But they were
sadly handicapped. They could scarcely denounce either
property as such or money-business as such. Their own

feudalism was a form of property. The Church itself was the biggest property-owner, and various Church organizations were virtually in the banking business.

Circumstances favored the growth of commercial power. But such power never rests on force alone. People tolerated the feudal order not so much because the nobles carried swords as because the whole thing was thought to express 'the law of God.' The merchants and their spokesmen of course denied this. They also asserted the rights and privileges of property. The classic refutation of divine right and counter-assertion of property right is that of the great English philosopher, John Locke, written in justification of the 'bloodless revolution' of 1688 in which his merchant friends in Parliament had unseated the Catholic Stuart king, James II, substituting the commerce-minded Dutch Protestant Prince of Orange as William III.

But denial of the other fellow's right is not enough, especially if you concede his grounds for believing in his right. Locke argued that it is property and not kings that expresses the law of God. But the Church and the feudal order had made the first claim. 'The law of God' was their monopoly.

Moreover, for any right to be effective it must be 'functional.' It must perform a real and important function in the society in which it exists, or at least seem to do so. Feudalism did this. For an agricultural society control of land is certainly functional. Since the land could be tilled only as the system authorized, it seemed as though the first consideration to the successful raising of crops was the blessing of the system.

Does money bestow a similar blessing? From medieval times onward that was the crucial question. Aristotle had declared that money does not breed, and the medieval

Church endorsed his reasoning. But, as we have seen, the medieval world already recognized property and money power. Consequently it could not denounce interest as such. The Church heaped its anathemas upon 'usury,' but it allowed exceptions: recompense for threatened loss, a share in the earnings of joint undertakings, and so on. And in doing so it gave its case away.

The historic argument over 'usury' tells the whole story. Obviously money does not breed. But it is equally obvious that power does. We recognize this great principle in the ancient and familiar proverb about an inch and an ell. In late medieval and early modern times industry and commerce were growing fast. For money power to displace feudal power and eventually rule the roost, all that was necessary was a functional relationship to industry and commerce. The Church's own theory of the 'silent partnership' of the investor was entirely sufficient.

In such a partnership the power element is always paramount. The feudal lord never put his hand to the plow, but it was he who seemingly 'made it possible' for others to do so. This is the function which money power assumed in commercial society. It is the grant of money power which seemingly 'makes possible' every industrial undertaking. The power to permit or forbid seems in effect to be the whole thing. Plows and serfs, machines and operatives, fade into the background as mere 'material agencies' of the real 'life force' of feudalism or of capitalism. This is what Louis XIV meant to assert, a little late in history, to be sure, when he exclaimed, 'The state is myself!' The identification of a sum of money with the business undertaking which it 'makes possible' has precisely the same meaning. The undertaking would in fact be checked if the sum were not granted, but that was also true of Louis's France.

In this way the great usury argument was settled in favor of capital about the middle of the sixteenth century. By that time the capitalists were in the saddle. A recent writer has cited a document dated 1559 to the effect that since the first act of Parliament under Henry VIII 'there could never been won any good law or order which touched [the merchants'] liberty or estate, but they stayed it.' One of the wisest and most learned interpreters of this century has said of it, 'A century before, businessmen had practiced extortion and been told that it was wrong; for it was contrary to the law of God. A century later [they were] to practice it and be told that it was right; for it was in accordance with the law of nature.'

Some people call it nature, but others call it capital. Even in early modern times industry was growing fast. That growth was a function of the industrial equipment of the community, as anybody could see even in early times. To identify that function with the accumulation of money was to attribute the whole thing to the men who made money. That is what we accomplish by calling both things 'capital.' The argument runs as follows: Economic progress results from the growth of the material equipment of industry, that is to say, capital; capital, that is to say, money, is created by 'saving'; therefore, economic progress is made possible by 'saving.' In this fashion the money power became functional.

This is the idea which was forming in the minds of the merchants and their spokesmen during the sixteenth century. The word 'capital' first begins to appear in economic writings just about the middle of that century. By the time of Locke it was a commonplace. By the time of Adam Smith it was a 'law of nature.' In our time it is so familiar that we are shocked to discover that every time we use the word 'capital' we are indulging in double-talk.

The double-talk of capital has become an ingrained habit. It runs through virtually every textbook. Textbook writers solemnly warn their students of the dangers of confusion which lurk behind this word. Resolutely they insist that it must be used to refer to one thing or the other, and not both. With exemplary clarity they declare, for example, that they propose to use it to refer only to the physical equipment of industry: plant, machines, raw materials, and so forth. And in the very next paragraph we find them saying that capital is brought into existence by saving! But now, obviously, they are talking about money!

That is how it is done.

3

The 'Spirit' of Capitalism

No ONE CAN DENY that the power of money is real. As things stand, 'there could never been won' any industrial undertaking without money authorization. This has been true throughout modern times. Consequently it is true that money power, the power system known as 'capitalism,' has played a part in bringing modern industrial society into existence. The question is, What part?

To answer this question we have to distinguish between types of causes. Logicians make a distinction between 'efficient' and 'sufficient' causes. That is, a thing may act 'efficiently' as a cause of something else without being 'sufficient' to bring that other thing into existence. Thus, lowered vitality is an 'efficient' cause of colds, but it is not 'sufficient' to account for your having a cold. Nobody can contract a cold except by infection from somebody else.

In the case of capitalism the difference is one of kind as well as of amount of influence. Low vitality offers no barrier to infection of any kind. It is thus a 'permissive' cause of whatever illness may ensue. But it is not 'creative' of your cold or other illness. The 'creative' cause is the infection.

In this sense capitalism was a permissive cause of many other changes, including industrial development. That it was the creative cause of the modern industrial system is certainly not true.

The disappearance of feudalism affected the whole of Western civilization. Old ties were loosened all along the line. We speak of this process as a growth of individualism. This seems to imply that a race of individuals somehow came into existence who refused to be bound by feudal ties and therefore burst them. Such a view is of course highly complimentary to the individuals concerned. The question is, Who were these individuals and how did they manage to get that way?

Some economic historians have tried to glorify the businessman in this fashion. The idea seems to be that businessmen were the first to begin to think rationally. One writer says that 'all logic is derived from the pattern of the economic decision,' and that 'the spirit of rationalist individualism, the spirit generated by rising capitalism,' was responsible for all the scientific and educational developments of modern times including even painting, literature, and so forth.

In that case, where did the business man get his genius? Some writers have offered the Protestant Reformation as the answer to this question. Because Protestantism gives great importance to the individual conscience, and because some Protestant divines urged their flocks to 'make more, save more, give more,' it is suggested that capitalist individualism began here.

But there is much evidence against these theories. The leaders of the Reformation began by trying to reform the Catholic Church and broke with it only after this effort failed. This break necessarily imposed a burden of responsibility upon individual conscience. But it was not the intention of the 'reformers' to sweep away every vestige of Catholicism. On the contrary, their disposition was to retain all they could of the traditional forms of organization and of worship. The oldest Protestant denominations still continue to do so.

Most historians insist that such was the case quite generally. The staunch burghers of the late medieval and early modern towns — ancestors of the modern bourgeoisie — were not revolutionists. On certain specific issues, such as taxation, they did oppose the lords and kings. They had to, for on these issues their own existence was at stake. On all other matters, however, they were quite conservative. It was not their intention to upset feudalism. Testimony is virtually unanimous on this point. If they were the great individualists, they at least were quite unaware of it.

Industry and thrift are not distinctively Protestant virtues. They are not even a capitalistic monopoly. Indeed, they are not even modern. Consider the industry and thrift with which Jacob labored for Rachel, the daughter of Laban! To attribute such virtues to Protestantism is to find an imaginary explanation of imaginary qualities.

The spirit of capitalism is the spirit of a power system based on property and expressed in the power of money. There is no question about the origin and character of that system. It was derived from an earlier power system, that of feudalism, and it continues the immemorial tradition by which communities are divided into the rulers and the ruled.

The question is whether money power as such brought the industrial system of machine production into existence.

There is only one reason for supposing that it did, the supposition that money power and machine production are identical, and that is an illusion of double meanings. If we ask the straight question, 'Was capitalism the creative cause of the growth of modern industry?' there can be only one answer: No.

It may be true that capitalism as a system is less rigid, or more flexible, than feudalism. It may be true that capitalism has been more hospitable to industrial growth than feudalism was or would have been had it persisted. It may even be true that many of the men who have wielded power under capitalism have favored science and invention and welcomed industrial innovations. But at the very most this means only that capitalism has been a permissive cause of industrial growth. As an institutional climate, it has perhaps been favorable.

But to suppose that moneymaking is the seed from which the whole of modern industrial society has sprung is to talk nonsense.

4

The Growth of Industry

Actually, MACHINE PRODUCTION is an outgrowth of science and invention. We all know that this is true of present developments. That is why science is held in such high esteem today, and that is why inventors are honored and rewarded.

How long has this been going on? Nearly everybody would agree that the situation has been much the same as it is now for at least two hundred years. The invention of the steam engine is commonly supposed to have ushered in the machine age. This invention did not occur alone, of course. By some strange chance, apparently, it was accompanied by a group of inventions in the field of spinning and weaving: the flying shuttle, which led to the power loom; the spinning jenny, Crompton's mule, and similar devices, which led to the complete mechanization of woolen manufacture; the cotton gin, which gave cotton an advantage over wool.

This machinery was set up in the first modern factories and so ushered in the factory system. The growth of new industrial centers drained population from the countryside and so started an unending series of social changes, all of

which is now identified as 'the industrial revolution.' It is
called a revolution, not in the sense of an armed revolt, but
in the more significant sense of a process of change, very extensive and profound, affecting the whole of Western society,
and still going on. This revolution is now universally recognized to be industrial; that is, scientific discoveries and industrial inventions have been the causes of all the changes. For
example, the automobile has changed the pattern of our
towns and has seriously affected family life and even church
attendance.

But how did the industrial revolution start? When did it
really begin? So dramatic was the appearance of the steam
engine that for a long time it seemed to have begun a new
era quite different from anything that had gone before. We
know very little about the early history of our machines. Nobody thought it of much importance. Even the history of
science was scandalously neglected. Scientists were always
more concerned with new discoveries, and historians with
wars and politics.

In the absence of positive knowledge, legend always continues to prevail. So long as nobody troubled to investigate
the early history of industry, the gap was filled by the familiar beliefs about 'the spirit of capitalism' and so on.
Recently, however, the situation has changed. During the
last few decades a great deal of work has been done in this
field, much more than all previous investigations put together. As a result, we now know positively that the industrial revolution did not begin with the steam engine, but has
been going on for a very long time.

All the epochal inventions of modern times derive from
similarly epochal scientific discoveries. The laws of the expansion of gases were discovered in the century preceding

the steam engine. That was the century not only of Boyle
and Hooke, but of Newton and Harvey, Huygens and
Galileo — a golden age of science. Furthermore, the relationship between science and industry is by no means a one-way
flow. Galileo's telescope and Hooke's microscope were both
products of what we should now call the optical glass industry. Science is just as dependent upon the industrial arts
and crafts as they are upon science. This golden age of science was itself preceded by an earlier golden age of invention and discovery.

It has often been said that the invention of printing was
the most significant event in European history. Viewed in a
setting of political and military history, its significance is
somewhat obscure. As a feature of the industrial revolution,
its meaning and importance are obvious. Not only is printing the carrier by which all discoveries and inventions are
spread abroad; still more important — it is the agent of literacy, and literacy as we now know is the foundation of industrial advancement.

Printing also contains a key to the whole enigma of industrial revolution. How did it happen? We know that the
ancient Chinese art of printing from wood blocks was introduced into Europe by the Mongols, whose conquests extended all the way from China to Poland. But the Chinese
had never developed movable types, and for a most com-
pelling reason. Chinese writing was not alphabetical. It
employed word-symbols so vast in number that interchange-
ability was quite impractical. In contrast, Europeans used
phonetic alphabets derived from Latin and Greek which in
turn got their alphabets from the Phoenicians. In all the
world, only this group of languages was alphabetical. But
these peoples had no art of printing. When the art of print-

ing was combined with the use of phonetic alphabets, a tremendous revolution occurred. For the first time in world history the general run of people learned to read and write. The stimulus this gave to industrial revolution was beyond our power to exaggerate.

Nevertheless, this was by no means the only incident of the kind. To give only two other examples, gunpowder and the compass have long been symbols of revolutionary change. Probably it was the metal trades that made the difference between Chinese firecrackers and European ordnance. Probably the astrolabe, by which latitude could be determined, was more important than the compass; and probably ships were more important than either. The voyages of the late fifteenth and early sixteenth century have always teased the imaginations of historians — they occurred so suddenly, and they had such prodigious consequences. All sorts of reasons for them have been invented, such as that old favorite 'the spirit of adventure.' But now it turns out that ships capable of carrying cargoes across oceans were built for the first time during the fifteenth century by combining the seaworthiness of the Viking ships with the superior construction and rigging of Mediterranean shipbuilders.

Industrial revolutions have been occurring as far back as we can see. The European society upon which such things as printing had such an explosive effect was itself the orphan child of a very ancient civilization. Some twelve to fifteen thousand years earlier agriculture had been developed along the fertile and well-protected valleys of the Near East. That, too, was one of the great industrial revolutions of all time, no less significant than the earliest use of fire and chipped flint. For agriculture is a stabilizer. It anchors a community in one spot where as a consequence of long-fixed residence material equipment of all kinds is accumulated. The three or four great civilizations of the world developed by slow accumulation along the Nile, Tigris, and Euphrates rivers, the Indus and the Ganges, the Hoang-ho and Yangtse-kiang, and wherever it was that corn was first domesticated in the New World.

Western Europe was the frontier of a tremendously old and rich Mediterranean culture. Thus, the iron age which Watt ushered in really began when the smelting of iron was discovered in what is now Turkey some time before the siege of Troy. The Romans conquered Gaul and brought all their tools and accoutrements, all their arts and all their knowledge of materials, across the Alps into their new province. Then they lost the province. It was not so much that Rome fell as that Gaul fell away. The Roman Empire persisted almost to the time of Columbus, but western Europe was not a part of it.

Thus, the freedom of the frontier was intensified by independence. We used to think of medieval civilization as utterly rigid and dogma-ridden, hidebound and traditionalized in every way; and so it was by comparison with modern Europe or America. But compared with the other great centers of culture at that time, European society was a brawling infant, far less tradition-ridden than China, or India, or Islam, or Byzantium. That is why contact with Islam or with China altered Europe so much more than it did Islam or China.

The Crusaders brought back the windmill and the water-wheel, and with them the germ of power-driven machinery. Islam gave Europe its science of arithmetic, the numerals it had borrowed from India, and the art of bookkeeping. China yielded printing. To those peoples the Europeans of that

day were 'outer barbarians.' Contact with Europe, and even
with each other, made little difference. For example, Islam
also had its chance to adopt Chinese printing. But the ten
commandments of the Mohammedan religion forbid 'graven
images,' and so the opportunity was lost. Europeans also
had their ancient scruples. But, as Americans should certainly be able to understand, on the frontier scruples give
way to manifest destiny.

Thus, western Europe became the scene of a long series of
industrial revolutions of which industrial society is the result. We who have witnessed the appearance of the automobile and the airplane know what a revolution in transportation means. But a French historian has found evidence
of a great revolution in transport brought about by the invention of the horse-collar and the development of wagons
and wagon roads about A.D. 1000, two centuries *before*
medieval civilization reached its height. An American historian has shown that the twelfth century, a century before
the pinnacle of medievalism, witnessed a great cultural revolution.

The evidence is clear. Industrial revolution is not a consequence of something else. It has been going on always.
What we see now is the last item of a continuous series of
inventions and discoveries of which the first was perhaps the
discovery of fire long before the evolution of the present
species of man.

5

The Social Dividend

FOR EVERY SOCIETY the most important economic fact is the size of the social dividend. Economists use the word 'dividend' in this connection to mean just what it means in arithmetic, namely, that which is to be divided. They have usually spoken of 'the national dividend,' meaning the entire product of all the efforts of a whole nation. But since this conception of a nation refers not so much to a government as to a people or society, it seems clearer to speak of the 'social' dividend.

With regard to the primary importance of the social dividend economists have always been unanimous, and for obvious reasons. Obviously it is the amount of the total product that determines the fate of a community. If the social dividend is less than the physical requirements of the community, famine is the inevitable result. If it is more than minimum physical requirements, then some measure of prosperity prevails.

In every famine some members of the community starve earlier than others. Some are always more prosperous than others. That is, every economic system performs a distributive function as well as a productive function. If one is called the dividend, the other might be called the divisor. But at this point the analogy to arithmetic breaks down. In arithmetic the size of the quotient is affected by any change in either divisor or dividend, but divisor and dividend do not affect each other. In our economic life, however, the reverse is true. Production and distribution do affect each other, directly and continuously. Thus, all students are agreed that the growth of the factory system of production so profoundly altered the distribution of income as to affect the balance of power of the classes in the industrial nations. Students are also agreed that the relatively high wages and standards of living of American labor have contributed mightily to the industrial growth of the United States.

Since distribution and production do condition each other, and since the size of the social dividend is of paramount importance, it follows that what is most important about any system of distribution is the effect it has on the production of the social dividend. That is why it was not enough to attribute the very great inequality of capitalism to 'the will of God.' The vital question has always been, What is its effect on production?

The orthodox capitalist answer to this question has always been that such a distributive system as the one we inherited from feudalism has been and is essential to industrial production; that the social dividend of industrial society is dependent upon such a distributive system. For industrial production is dependent upon the supply of capital, the supply of capital is dependent upon saving, and saving is dependent upon inequality of incomes.

The whole issue thus turns upon this conception of production. If this conception is unsound, if the realities of industrial production are not what this argument supposes, then the soundness of capitalism itself is open to question. For if the real causes of industrial growth are science and invention, the spread of literacy and scientific enlightenment to the whole community and the gradual acquisition by the community of industrial skills, then industrial advancement is a community affair in the broadest possible sense. All the activities of the community, educational and cultural as well as those which are narrowly scientific and industrial, contribute to the common undertaking. No single individual and no particular group has any clear priority in this general process. It has happened over and over again that the work of some obscure and neglected scientist has later turned out to be indispensable to the community effort, just as the waste products of the past have later turned out to be the indispensable materials of new scientific or industrial developments.

We now know that such is indeed the case. The social dividend of industrial society is the creation of the whole community. The supposition that this social process is dependent upon the accumulation of sums of money by a distributive system calculated to perform that function is a fantastic error. That system is indeed a source of power. But it is not the source of the social dividend.

This does not mean that the capitalist system of distribution has no effect on industrial production. It may even have an ill effect. Indeed, the evidence is now conclusive that it does.

6

Saving vs. Consumption

SAVING is the cardinal virtue of capitalist society. For several centuries it has been linked in sermon, song, and edifying tale with the staunch Puritan virtues of decency, sobriety, and self-respect. Those who think of Christianity as the foundation of capitalism think of this virtue as the foundation stone.

This conception of saving is typical of the double-talk by which economic discussion has been plagued. For if anything in the field of economics is definitely and positively known, it is that nearly all saving is involuntary. Virtue has little or nothing to do with it. We save because we have no choice. It is a statistical fact, many, many times substantiated, that individual savings vary directly with incomes. The very poor save nothing — indeed, less than nothing, since they consume the savings of the more fortunate. The very rich save most of their incomes, not because they are more abstemious than other people, but because, with all their ingenuity and determination and with the practiced help of expert advisers, they are still unable to stand the strain of spending more than a small part of their millions.

A great deal of saving is done by financial institutions, and some of these are savings banks and insurance companies which pool the small savings of many individual clients. Such persons may indeed be praiseworthy as compared with their less provident neighbors. But their individual virtue does not extend to the system. For it must not be forgotten that saving to provide for one's old age or for the education of one's children is still involuntary in a society which makes no other provision for old age or education.

Moreover, saving is presumed to be an economic virtue for quite a different reason. Saving is non-consumption. Puritan morality praises self-restraint and frowns upon excessive consumption on the theory that it is inherently bad. But obviously that is not good economics. Since the consumer is the ultimate market for all goods and services, a general curtailment of consumption can only mean a general reduction of the market for everybody's goods and services. Total nonconsumption would mean the total collapse of the demand for goods and services. No economist has ever advocated anything of this kind. Not even the slightest degree of curtailment of demand is expected to result from the economic function of saving. The whole idea is not to reduce the total volume of consumption, but to divert part of the flow of goods and services to investment channels.

This is a very strange idea. Let us suppose that an agricultural community decides to build a railroad. It is pretty obvious that eating less is not the answer. However much people may tighten their belts, rails and locomotives are not made of wheat and turnips. If the railroad is to be built, some considerable number of men hitherto engaged in farming must go to mining and smelting iron, rolling steel, and fabricating rails and engines. But these men must eat, and it is impossible for them to take the food out of the mouths of the remainder of the community. The demand for food, as we say, is relatively inelastic. No community has ever been willing to suffer — none has in fact ever suffered — any absolute reduction such as would be involved in this instance.

What people have been willing to forego is greater abundance. Industrial progress increases the efficiency of farming, making it possible for more crops to be produced by fewer men. But eating habits are relatively fixed. Therefore, instead of raising and eating more food, we have diverted men from agriculture into industry where also industrial revolution has been going on, so the new industries have been springing up into which men have been absorbed. That is really how railroads have been built.

It has been proved again and again that industrial equipment is not produced at the expense of consumers' goods. On the contrary, more consumers' goods are produced at the very time and place of an increase in the production of industrial equipment. That is what happened in America during the Second World War. It is exactly what we should expect on the supposition that industrial growth is by the process known as industrial revolution, and it is directly contrary to the capitalist doctrine of saving.

But the whole idea of building railroads by eating less is an afterthought. The original capitalist notion has nothing to do with either bread or rails. Rather it views the whole operation in terms of money. Obviously what is saved is money. And what does it take to build railroads? To the capitalist mind the answer to this question is no less obvious and simple: again, money. Money which is not spent by the general public for consumers' goods is invested by capitalists in additional plant.

Now investment is a form of spending. We always call it 'government spending' when money is being invested by a government agency. On the assumption that every dollar that is saved is promptly invested, no great harm is done. It only means that a shift of funds is running parallel to the shift of men and materials into new industries. To be sure, control of the saving and investment process means control of the new industries. But that is neither new nor catastrophic — provided all that is 'saved' is promptly spent investmentwise.

It would indeed be catastrophic if such were not the case. For in that event the total flow of purchasing power would be reduced. Not enough dollars would be finding their way into the market by one channel or the other to buy the entire product of industry. With this drop in total demand, production would have to be curtailed. Men would be laid off and orders for materials would be canceled, so that the flow of purchasing power would be further reduced, and so on to disaster.

Economists have been aware of this terrible danger for many years. A few heretics have even tried to warn us that it was imminent. But the true believers have always insisted that it was impossible. For, they have argued, what moves men to save is the prospect of getting interest on their money. If the demand for investment funds were to slacken, that would automatically lower the interest rate, which after all is only the premium enterprisers pay for funds. This would automatically check saving, and so the balance would be restored. The presumption apparently is that people would forthwith eat more and save less.

What this argument overlooks is the curious character of 'saving,' and perhaps that is why orthodox capitalist thinking has clung so tenaciously to that misleading word. If 'saving' were Puritan abstemiousness translated into funds, such an automatic adjustment might conceivably occur. There would still be some ground for misgiving as to whether it would happen fast enough to be effective. That, indeed, is what economists have mostly argued about. But if 'saving' is not a matter of abstemiousness at all — and we know that it is not — if it is in fact a consequence of a distributive system in which some incomes are unspendable, then what we call 'saving' is going to continue quite irrespective of the interest rate. Even the small-scale saver who is laying by a nestegg for his old age is going to have to save more if he sees his nestegg dwindling.

The whole situation becomes perfectly clear if we view money as the medium of power, as indeed we should. Ours is a money economy in the sense that money is power. This is true for the man of limited means no less than for the greatest capitalist. It is by accumulating money that one establishes his sons in the professions and the other extends his control over additional industries. The motive in both cases is entirely independent of the interest rate or any other expression of the needs or wishes of society.

That such a motive should not lead to overaccumulation would be miraculous. We know now that it does. Evidence has been compiled to show that the rate of accumulation was accelerating throughout the supposed prosperity of the nineteen-twenties, reaching a climax in 1929, when three times as much money was accumulated in the United States as could be absorbed by real industrial expansion. This money bought nothing. Having been diverted from the incomes of the masses who might have spent it, this immense sum, roughly six billions of dollars, was laid out in inflated security values by a process of pseudo-investment. Thus, the American economy was deprived of a market for its goods and services to a degree sufficient to plunge the whole country into the depression of the nineteen-thirties.

All this is highly disturbing. In the face of these facts it is impossible to maintain that saving and investment are always equal and that the automatic adjustments of the price system always provide a market for the entire product of industry. During the nineteen-thirties, while unsold goods were piling up in warehouses for all the world to see, economists made a very upsetting discovery. They discovered that saving and investment are not identical and not even necessarily equal. This was the most unsettling economic discovery of modern times. It has fluttered the academic dovecotes far more than all the bitter sarcasms of Marx and all the recondite ironies of Veblen.

For it means the utter collapse of the whole elaborate structure of ideas by which capitalism has justified itself. It means that the distributive system to which industrial society has submitted is wholly without justification. Not only is it not a blessing in disguise; it is the wellspring of all economic evil, the curse of Adam upon industrial society.

7

Depression

No ADULT now living needs to be convinced that depression is a fact. We have just witnessed a depression of such magnitude that it seemed to threaten the existence of industrial society itself and perhaps still does through its aftermath of war and revolution. Indeed, many are saying that the next depression is just around the corner.

We know that depressions have occurred from time to time throughout the past. The evidence on this point is overwhelming. All students of the subject accept it as an established fact. In recent years an immense amount of statistical work has been done in the attempt to find out whether depressions occur at regular intervals and, if so, what the intervals are. The information so acquired is, of course, exceedingly important and valuable. Nevertheless, the tremendous emphasis which has thus been placed on the periodicity of booms and slumps has had a most unfortunate effect.

Early nineteenth-century economists denied the possibility of general and prolonged stagnation such as we have witnessed during the nineteen-thirties. But it was impossible for them to deny the existence of slumps. Consequently they argued that a slump is a 'deflationary movement' which lets the hot air out of the preceding 'inflationary move-ment,' thus restoring the economic balance. Emphasis upon the periodicity of prosperity and depression naturally serves to nourish this state of mind.

By imperceptible degrees anyone who thinks in these terms gets into the habit of thinking of each upward move-ment as the cause of the ensuing downward movement, and vice versa, just as one might think of each swing of a pen-dulum as the cause of the opposite swing, ignoring such ques-tions as what set the pendulum swinging in the first place and what sort of mainspring keeps it perpetually in motion. The supposition is that each swing 'generates' the ensuing opposite swing, and that is all there is to it.

This is known as the 'self-generating' theory. Really it is not a theory at all, only the standardization of ignorance. But as such it is extremely dangerous. Ignorance is a mis-fortune at all times, but when it is revered as dogma it be-comes a major calamity. This is the state of mind which pre-vailed in the early nineteen-thirties when men in positions of the gravest responsibility solemnly assured us all that nothing need be done about the depression, since it would inevitably lead to a recurrence of prosperity, which therefore was 'just around the corner.' There are some in whom this habit still persists today and who are therefore already talking of the depression which will 'inevitably' follow postwar inflation, which with admirable consistency they also think of as inevitable.

But pendulum thinking is not as common as it was. We have learned a lot since 1929. Obviously that is because we **have seen** a lot. So long as disturbances are kept within decent bounds, economists prefer to view them with Olympian detachment, taking a 'long-run' view of upward and downward movements and not worrying too much about incidental 'friction.' But when the friction generates heat so intense that it threatens to blow the whole outfit galleywest, most of us are strongly moved to stop, look, and listen.

What we have learned as a result now seems obvious indeed. The economic heretics have been trying all along to make us see it. No economy could swing back and forth so wildly from one extreme to the other without there being something very wrong about it. There is indeed something very wrong with ours. It fails to distribute mass-consumer purchasing power in sufficient quantity to permit the entire product of industry to be purchased. This failure exists at all times under capitalism and is noxious at all times. But the symptoms of the failure appear irregularly and in apparently contrasting sets.

This is true for reasons which are now well understood. Businessmen are obliged to anticipate their market. When they have reason to believe the market is going to expand, they must plan to increase production, if necessary by adding to their plant. Otherwise their competitors will hog the market. When they have reason to believe the market is going to contract, they must cancel whatever plans for expansion they may have had. Otherwise they will be stuck with excess plant capacity.

This means that construction industries are a feast-or-famine proposition. Since everybody wants additional plant at the same time, and everybody cancels orders for plant at the same time, the industries which supply the basic plant, tools, and materials to other industry are either crowded to capacity or in a state of complete suspension.

These industries themselves employ a large labor force whose wages constitute an appreciable fraction of the total flow of consumer purchasing power. When this stream of purchasing power is flowing at full flood, it constitutes a substantial market for the goods and services of the whole economy, and when it is dried up, the whole economy feels the check. Consequently this behavior of the basic construction goods industries strongly accentuates any upward or downward movement.

In recent years there has been much discussion of the 'multiplier,' as this factor in the economic process is now generally called. So great is its importance in explaining the succession of periods of prosperity and depression that many have succumbed to the temptation of thinking that if only the multiplier could be controlled, all would be well. But this overlooks the fact that it is only the symptoms that are multiplied.

If our economy were constitutionally sound, the expansion which accompanies prosperity would not be unwholesome and dangerous. But it is not sound. The real disease is constitutional. Even in periods of prosperity the flow of mass-consumer purchasing power fails to keep pace with the growth of industry. Hence the accentuation of this movement by the multiplier is dangerous.

This was true, for example, throughout the nineteen-twenties. That was the 'new era.' There was much talk of the 'discovery' that high wages pay off in prosperity. The flow of mass-consumer purchasing power was indeed increasing throughout the decade. But we now know that it was not increasing anything like as fast as the national income. On the contrary, the discrepancy between mass purchasing power and total productive capacity was steadily increasing from 1922 to 1929. At the peak, in the early months of 1929 — as the Brookings Institution showed in its justly famous studies of America's capacity to produce and consume — production was nineteen per cent short of existing capacity.

We may never know why the crash came in October, 1929, or what specific incidents brought it on just at that moment. But we do know that such incidents and dates are of minor importance. As a few people had already seen, such a crash was bound to come sooner or later. For three years depression deepened, with production steadily falling off, and unemployment of men and dollars steadily increasing, until in the winter of 1932-33 an avalanche of bank failures had begun.

At this point a new administration began to pay out mass-consumer purchasing power. It was a mere trickle at first, but its effect was instantaneous. The flow increased continuously until the winter of 1936-37, when the soldiers' bonus was pyramided on top of the payments of the various recovery agencies. What immediately followed was a sharp upturn of prosperity.

No doubt the sharpness of this upturn was accentuated by the multiplier. It was generally appreciated at the time that the upward movement of early 1937 was in considerable part an 'inventory boom.' That is, businessmen were inspired by the first signs of recovery to hope for full prosperity, which they anticipated accordingly by stocking all their shelves.

But this boom had the inevitable political effect. Economic heretics had long ago declared that with the first signs of returning prosperity businessmen would throw all the medicine out of the window. Strong pressure was brought on Congress to stop all pump-priming nonsense.

Consequently the flow of purchasing power was sharply checked, and the recession of late 1937 was the instantaneous result. This, of course, led to a resumption of 'pump-priming,' and a resumption of moderate recovery.

But it was not recovery measures that ended the depression. It was the war. Spokesmen of 'free private enterprise' who are most bitter in their denunciation of all the 'utopian nonsense' about 'spending our way out of depression' are most insistent upon this point. But in their eagerness to discredit the government program, they overlook a fact of the greatest significance. As all economists recognize, war is a colossal system of outdoor relief, a gigantic public-works program. Industry boomed during the war. The volume of production reached undreamed-of heights. And the whole thing was financed by government funds.

If this flow of funds is simply turned off, and especially if stored-up purchasing power is drained off by inflation, the result will be a depression as much deeper than the last as our war production was greater than that of 1929.

An uneasy awareness of that prospect is now insinuating itself into many minds. As long as we possibly can, we will think in terms of gratitude to the returning soldier rather than in terms of the necessity of continuing the flow of mass-consumer purchasing power. For we are not yet ready to admit that capitalism has failed. We fear the consequences of such admission.

That is why businessmen are so bitter in their denunciation of government spending. In recent years they have often been reproached for lack of gratitude. It has been pointed out repeatedly that the bitterest and most articulate among them are the very bankers who were saved from extinction in 1933 by the very administration they have castigated ever since. This is not lack of gratitude. It is an act of faith, faith in the sense of 'believin' what you know ain't so.' The calm assurance of earlier and happier days has given way to hysterical reiteration of dogmas that are no longer self-evident. The failure of capitalism to maintain the flow of mass-consumer purchasing power that is necessary to sustain the industrial economy is now established, and that is most upsetting.

Moreover, it is by no means the end of the story. For this failure is also the cause of war and revolution.

8

War

THAT CAPITALISM SUFFERS from a chronic deficiency of consumer purchasing power has never been generally admitted. But it does 'need markets.' That has been understood since early modern times.

Furthermore, the need has been for markets for the exports of the capitalist nations. That also has been clearly understood since early modern times. That is what the Mercantilists meant by a 'favorable' balance of trade. It is what the empire-builders definitely intended to secure from their colonial empires. That economic 'necessity' is what has driven the capitalist nations into war. As Hitler truly said in one of his rare moments of candor, 'Germany must export or die.' So, indeed, must every capitalist nation.

This grim necessity has nothing to do with any particular commodity or type of commodities. War has focused public attention upon strategic raw materials. But raw materials are not the prime cause of the disorder. Indeed, raw materials do not become strategic until war is imminent. A man does not attack his neighbor in order to get hold of a weapon with which to protect himself from him, nor does a nation go to war to secure the means of making war. No nation has ever controlled all the strategic raw materials, and short of conquering the earth no nation could do so. For one thing, the essential raw materials of future wars are as yet unknown. What are the essential materials of the weapons that have not yet been invented? How much did the Army War College worry about aluminum and hundred-octane gasoline before 1940? What were the War Department plans for magnesium before 1942? To judge by the size of the national stock-pile, even rubber was the occasion for little concern before December 7, 1941.

The truth is, access to raw material has never been a serious economic problem. Such things are imports, and the problem of imports has always been not to get them, but to keep them out. No nation has ever kept imports out altogether. Whatever the domestic economy fails to provide may be permitted to enter, in moderate quantities. But no nation has ever welcomed imports, not even England in the palmiest days of free trade.

For imports compete with domestic production. In the case of a well-furnished economy like that of the United States this means virtually everything. During the recent depression the United States presented to the world the strange spectacle of a community suffering from overproduction of manufactured goods of all kinds and simultaneously of the entire range of farm products and industrial raw materials. It was indeed a case of starvation in the midst of plenty.

This is the situation which provides the urge to export, since to do so is to shift the burden of depression to the foreigner. This is true even when he gets a bargain, since every sale gives a modicum of domestic employment and so

permits a modicum of purchasing power to flow into the
domestic market. Any firm which is able to control the
prices of its products with the aid of advertising and 'Fair-
Trade' laws may find it profitable to offer the same goods to
foreigners for a fraction of the domestic price. If the domestic sale is adequate to cover the overhead costs, foreign sales
need be limited only by current costs.

Indeed, the whole nation may go on the bargain counter
by the simple expedient of cheapening its currency. In this
way the foreigner may be offered five dollars' worth of as-
sorted exports in exchange for four dollars' worth of whatever imports are not excluded by protective tariffs. In some
cases it has been considerably less.

This, of course, is economic warfare. Throughout modern
times the capitalist nations have used all the expedients at
their command, and always for the same purpose: to force
upon foreign markets the goods which their domestic pop-
ulations were unable to buy.

In this fantastic scramble the construction industries have
once more played a strategic part. It may be difficult to sell
the barefoot peoples shoes even at cut rates, except in the
stories of O. Henry where it is done with cockleburs. But
railways can be built anywhere. The reason for this is that
shoes are sold to individual purchasers who are no better
provided with purchasing power in tropical countries than
elsewhere — indeed, rather worse. But railways are sold to
governments, or at least to corporations, and in either case
the sale may be financed by loans. And this also is a boon
to suffering capitalism.

For it must never be forgotten that capitalism accumu-
lates funds. Since the whole justification for the system
turns on the dire need for such funds, politeness forbids us

ever to speak of overaccumulation. It is rather a dearth of 'investment opportunities' in the domestic economy that has made foreign investment a perennial need. We have goods that cannot be sold, and money that cannot be invested. What more obvious than that we should lend the foreigner the money wherewith to buy our goods?

The bonds of foreign governments and foreign corporations, duly sponsored by their governments and our own, provide the ideal machinery for this transaction. Our manufacturer of railway equipment or cotton-mill machinery does not himself accept such bonds in payment. The bonds are sold to our harassed investors to whom they bring welcome relief, and the manufacturers are paid in cash.

But the relief is only temporary. In due course the bonds are defaulted. This is very distressing to the individual investors who therefore press the government to call out the Marines. At this point economic warfare may pass into war. But we must not let this untoward eventuality blind us to the fact that getting rid of the funds altogether is a real relief. It means that the goods exported by virtue of those funds were from the point of view of the community a gift. Orators who declaim against the 'globaloney' of delivering milk to Hottentots would do well to figure up the total amount of our past munificence before committing themselves too finally.

The real tragedy is that the railways, the cotton mills, and all the rest of the industrial equipment with which we have endowed the less fortunate peoples not only remain but straightway go into business in competition with us. Alas, the number of continents to be spanned with railways is limited, and — worse still — so is the purchasing power of the world community. For many years the heavy industry of

Great Britain was able to contribute to the development of North America. Later the industrialization of Germany afforded a similar opportunity for capitalist beneficence. So, still later, did Japan. But not only was the absorptive capacity of these markets, and similar ones in South Africa, India, Australia, South America, and elsewhere, soon exhausted; the growth of industry in these regions imposed a steadily heavier burden on the purchasing capacity of the world.

The same is true of the great open spaces. One of the recurring symptoms of the capitalist malady is unemployment. It was the frontier which was chiefly responsible for the relief of unemployment in the past. So long as public lands remained on which the worthy poor might reasonably expect to sustain life more or less in the accustomed manner and might hope to grow up with the country to eventual affluence, such things as social security could remain in abeyance.

These opportunities were never evenly distributed. Perhaps that is why social-security plans appeared earlier in countries such as Germany which came late to the colonial feast. Certainly it is the reason for the cry of 'Lebensraum' which the 'have-not' nations have lately raised. Their need is genuine. But it is a requirement of the capitalistic system, not a physical necessity. This must be remembered in extenuation of the inconsistency with which the leaders of those peoples also preach the glories of fecundity. In a world of continuous economic warfare, it is inevitable that population also should be treated as a weapon.

Even for the luckiest 'haves' the advantage is limited. Frontiers disappear. It has taken the industrial peoples an amazingly short time to spread through all the open spaces which are climatically available for homesteading. There is no other region, apparently, in which a population such as that of the United States can be similarly placed.

In a very definite sense capitalism has reached the end of its bonanza period. The disorders of the twentieth century are the inevitable consequence.

The wars of the twentieth century may be the death agony of capitalism. But war serves also to prolong the agony. For the great deficiency of capitalism, underconsumption, is fully corrected by war. War absorbs all the surpluses and challenges production to exert its powers to the fullest. Full employment both of men and of funds becomes a reality under the consumptive stimulus of war. Industrial growth assumes dreamlike proportions, and the 'multiplier' works like magic.

That is why we regard war with mixed feelings. Because it corrects the fatal defect of capitalism, it appears in the guise of an economic boon. Industry is going full blast. Everybody is employed. Everybody is making money. The faintest whisper of peace puts the stock exchange into a dither. Nevertheless, war is bad, and not only because every family has sons on the fighting fronts. As a mode of consumption war is unconcealably and unequivocally bad. For as everyone can see, it is sheer destruction.

Consequently the perpetuation of capitalism by deliberate periodic recourse to war is an impossibility. Wartime production affords a measure of the enormity of the defect of capitalism. This, obviously, is the way we could run our industry if we could manage to consume on a scale commensurate with that of war. Sooner or later all this is bound to be apparent to the whole community, and when this happens the community will see that consumption in war is the price we pay for non-consumption in peace. But non-consumers never really favor non-consumption. Consequently when this time comes the day of capitalism will be over.

9

Revolution

Wₕₑₙ will the day of reckoning come? Where will the first outbreak occur? Who will fire the first shot?

No one knows the answers to these questions. Revolution follows no set pattern. The greatest revolution of modern times, perhaps the greatest in all history, was the one which produced the Soviet Union. The founders of the U.S.S.R. have all acknowledged the leadership of the greatest revolutionary theorist of all time, Karl Marx. But the evidence is conclusive that the Russian Revolution was not the result of Marxist agitation. Indeed, the leading Bolsheviki were not even present in Russia when the first outbreak occurred. Furthermore, Marxist theory pointed to the most highly industrialized centers as the scene of proletarian outbreaks, whereas in fact the Bolshevik Revolution occurred in the least industrialized country of Europe.

Nevertheless, all revolutions do seem to have one thing in common. All seem to be the result of extreme exasperation. This exasperation is a compound of two elements. One is severe and widespread misery. Obviously revolutions occur only when things have gone wrong on a gigantic scale. But misery alone is not enough. History affords many instances of the most grievous misery in which the revolutionary spirit seemed to be completely absent. This has sometimes been explained on the ground of the extremity of misery, and it is obvious that the spirit of revolution cannot flourish in an atmosphere of utter hopelessness. Thus, it has sometimes been said that revolutions occur only when things are getting better.

But why should anyone revolt when things are getting better? Every revolt is an uprising *against* somebody — against some human authority. Probably the most extreme misery is that of famines and plagues. But people do not revolt against hunger or disease. Neither do they revolt when the disease has run its course or when favorable weather conditions have brought a renewal of food and strength.

But when widespread and severe misery is plainly seen to be the direct consequence of the stupidity and frivolity of human agencies, then revolt is imminent. Thus, the second element of the exasperation from which revolutions flow is loss of moral authority.

The most disturbing feature of the great depression of the nineteen-thirties was the armed rebellion of the farmers. These men had gone bankrupt through no fault of their own. They had worked harder than ever and had produced good crops. But what they got for their crops was not sufficient to meet the payments on their mortgages. Consequently, when the mortgages were foreclosed and the farms put up at auction, the farmers' patience gave way, and they gathered at these auctions armed with shotguns and pitchforks with the announced intention of attacking anybody who ventured to bid against the present owners of the farms.

Very fortunately, this incident passed without serious trouble. Local authorities wisely refrained from attempting to enforce laws which had become unenforceable, and governmental agencies were set up which brought the farmers a considerable measure of relief.

This illustrates another aspect of the problem. When any given set of laws or institutions have lost their moral authority, the imminence of revolution seems to depend on the degree of rigidity or flexibility of those laws and institutions. Judicious change, such as the acceptance of the principle of limited monarchy by William and Mary, may restore the moral authority of the altered institution. Stubborn refusal may precipitate revolutionary violence, as refusal of the government of George III to abandon its colonial policy precipitated the American Revolution and refusal of the government of Louis XVI to accept the fiscal reforms offered by Turgot precipitated the French Revolution.

What is our present situation? Is the moral authority of capitalism unimpaired? Is there no danger of grievous misery? Are the institutions of capitalism sufficiently flexible to repair any threatened miseries and regain any threatened loss of moral authority?

For something like four centuries capitalism has owed its existence to the conviction, shared by rich and poor alike, that all parts of the community, workers no less than owners, owe to this system their present well-being and their hope of improvement.

In this respect capitalism is, of course, no different from all other power systems. What impelled the feudal villeins to accept their lot was an identical conviction. That conviction found expression in ideas and in language so fantastic as to seem to us utterly incredible. Looking back on the be-

liefs of medieval society, we wonder that anybody could
ever have believed such stuff.

The trouble is, we fail to look back far enough. There
was a time when men, who were not only quite free but
were also in a small way owners of land, sought out some
neighboring baron and persuaded him to take over their
lands and to accept them as loyal followers. The baron himself might be little more than a brigand, making no preten-
sions whatever to being God's anointed representative.
That made no difference. In those 'dark ages' no isolated
farmstead was safe. To survive at all a man had to join a
band. If he was a mighty man of valor, he might form a
band of his own and found a dynasty. If not, he must accept
the inevitable.

In the course of a few centuries the descendants of the
original war-lord get pretty well habituated to thinking of
themselves as very special people designated from on high
to lord it over their inferiors. Such a belief may be respected
by the whole community for a long time, as it was in the
case of feudalism. That is due in part to the fact that designation from on high is conceived in terms that are familiar
and acceptable to the whole community — in the case of
feudalism, those of Christian theology. But it will also be
due in considerable part to a sort of racial memory of the
situation in which the common man did indeed owe his very
existence to his relation to his liege lord. So long as any
trace of the original situation continues to persist — and that
was a long time in the case of medieval feudalism — that
sense of real common interest will also persist.

Every power system, however brutal, owes its existence to
the consent of the governed; and every superstition owes its
credibility to some demonstrable fact. Savages who submit

to having their own children offered up as living sacrifices in the magic rites of rain-making seem to us to have no sense of fact at all. It has even been suggested in all seriousness that their 'mentality' is 'pre-logical.' But this only means that in our relative security we have overlooked what is to them a basic fact. As a community they are utterly dependent upon the weather. Their awareness of this reality is so vivid that no sacrifice seems to them too great when measured against the enormity of general starvation. They are irrational for exactly the same reason that fear of cancer leads many of us into follies of credulity and superstition. Cancer at least is very real.

What is it that supports belief in capitalism? To get a realistic answer to this question we have only to recall the origin of modern Western society. Modern commercialism did not evolve out of feudal society. It grew first in the cracks and joints and crevices of the feudal order — that is, in the medieval towns and faubourgs which lay quite literally outside the manorial community. With the growth of the towns a struggle developed between the commercial town-dwellers — the 'bourgeoisie' — and the feudal community. Eventually the towns outgrew the feudal order and came to dominate the whole of society, giving to it the urbanism, the industrialism, and the commercialism which have been its distinguishing characteristics ever since.

In this struggle the whole town community stood together. Artisans and apprentices, rich merchants, powerful master journeymen, and common stevedores, all cast their lot together against the feudal society to which their communities were a challenge and a threat. Wherever feudal authority triumphed over a town community, the whole town suffered; and wherever a town grew and came to dominate the feudal countryside, the whole town profited.

This was a real solidarity. As such it was deeply appreciated by the whole urban community. Moreover, the struggle between these two types of society was long-drawn-out. To some extent it is still going on, and to that extent the common interest of owners and workers is a reality.

It was this common interest to which the idea of capital has seemed to give expression. Obviously that idea is not a literal description of the actual fact of 'bourgeois' (that is, townish) solidarity, any more than the idea of divine ordination is a literal description of the situation in which lords and serfs were in fact mutually dependent. Both ideas were taken from the ideological stock-piles of their communities, and consequently both exhibit all the merits and defects of the stock from which they issued. Both had the advantage of easy credibility. Divine ordination was a simple and obvious idea to the children of the medieval Church, and the identity of capital funds with capital equipment was no less simple and obvious to their descendants. The remark has often been made that capitalism is a sort of religion. That is literally true. Capital is a double-meaning concept in the same sense in which the Holy Trinity is a triple-meaning concept. To the late medieval mind there was nothing difficult or unnatural in such an idea.

But the foundation of every such belief is the actual situation — the demonstrable fact — to which it gives a sort of poetic expression. When that situation disappears, nothing is left to sustain the belief but the poetry which is increasingly remote from actuality and therefore begins to seem more and more fantastic. The resulting skepticism is one of the most conspicuous symptoms of revolutionary change. As every schoolboy knows, England experienced such symptoms in the seventeenth century, France in the eighteenth century.

We are now living in such a period. The basic actualities of the present situation are gradually becoming obvious to all. The capitalist creed did give expression to a common interest that was once a genuine reality. But that reality — the common cause of merchants and artisans against feudal authority — has long since disappeared. Nothing now remains of that ancient struggle but its watchwords, and they are fantastically remote from current actuality, two features of which are now emerging into general view. One is the machine. In the twentieth century for the first time the whole community has become machine-minded. It is now clear, as it has never been before, in what sense industrial society depends upon capital — that of machines and mechanical and scientific know-how. The other conspicuous feature of our economy is poverty in the midst of plenty. It is increasingly clear that the curtailment of consumer purchasing power in the interest of accumulation of funds for investment is not the open-sesame to industrial progress. On the contrary, it is water in the gas and sand in the bearings.

The facts are plain. Many people see them already, and it is only a question of time until everybody sees them. It is likewise only a question of time until another depression supplies the other ingredient of revolutionary exasperation. When that happens — when our persistence in a Bourbon capitalism, knowing nothing and forgetting nothing — brings an extremity of misery as much greater than that of the nineteen-thirties as our wartime level of production has been higher than that of 1929, will the community forget its disillusionment and submit meekly as though to the workings of an inscrutable providence? Only a Bourbon could believe it will.

Or will capitalism adjust itself to a changing world? Will

absolute capitalism give way to limited capitalism, as absolute monarchy gave way to limited monarchy, in England and elsewhere? The answer to this question depends on many things. But most of all it depends on our common understanding of what such a modification of capitalism would involve. This is the task to which the following chapters are addressed.

Part II

THE FLOW OF INCOME

10

So What?

ABSOLUTE CAPITALISM is doomed. It is doomed because its sole justification is a myth, and because the consequences of the myth are known to be calamitous.

People will tolerate a myth that does nobody any harm. They will not long tolerate a myth which has been discovered to be the prime cause of general and severe distress.

But what is the alternative?

This question is not an invitation to prophesy. Society is a large and complicated affair. Many problems confront us at many different points. There are many different trends upon the outcome of which various features of future society necessarily depend. No one can possibly understand all of them, or even know of their existence, and consequently it is quite futile to attempt to predict what climate of opinion will prevail in the future or what the institutional topography of future society will be.

All social problems are more or less interrelated. Any considerable economic change is bound to have repercussions some of which will be remote and even unpredictable. But this does not mean that any change at any point in the social structure is bound to result in the total alteration of the entire structure. After all, some institutions are more fundamental than others. No doubt abolition of the family, if we can imagine such a thing, would have very serious effects on every part of our whole civilization.

Is capitalism the foundation stone — the economic bedrock — on which the whole of modern civilization rests? That is how many people think of it. At this point, they think, any change at all is liable to bring the whole structure of organized society tumbling about our ears. An associate justice of the Supreme Court of the United States provided an historic example of this way of thinking only a few years ago. In delivering his lone dissenting opinion in the 'gold clause case' he said in effect that to nullify the clause by which corporations were bound to redeem their bonds in gold would mean the destruction of organized society. Even at the time this declaration gave more of an impression of emotional hysteria than of judicious analysis of causes and effects. But that state of mind is still uncomfortably common. A great many people talk of 'the attack on capitalism' as if the result of any successful 'attack' must necessarily mean the destruction of religion, the liquidation of the family, the end of all decent and comfortable living, and the nullification of every sort of personal integrity.

There is no logic by which people who have got into this condition can be disabused of such illusions. Their state of mind is quite impervious to logic. Theirs is the same shocked horror which some people experienced at the 'nationalization of women' by the Soviet Revolution of 1917. People 'knew' this awful thing must be so because of their horror and detestation of the Bolsheviki who, they 'knew,' were 'capable of anything.' Furthermore, they had the testimony of men of the highest honor and strongest sense of public responsibility, reported by the very papers that were most conspicuous for sobriety of utterance. These, in turn, 'knew' that what they were reporting must be true, since this was proved by the readiness of their readers to believe it. At the present time we know that it was all quite false. But all that is ancient history now, and ancient history is no safeguard against a fresh attack of hysteria. Alas, the same sort of witnesses are now engaged in telling us through the columns of the very same papers that any deviation from capitalist orthodoxy is a step down the road that leads to all the horrors of dictatorship.

If the end of capitalism comes in an atmosphere of mass hysteria, it is quite true that anything may happen. But to those who are still capable of reasoning, it should be obvious that no real occasion for alarm exists except what is provided by our own folly. Capitalism is not the oldest of human institutions. On the contrary, it is a fairly recent concoction. Moses did not receive it on Mount Sinai direct from the hand of God. Other societies, such as those of Greece and Rome, which perhaps achieved a good deal in their humble way, nevertheless managed to carry on without benefit of capitalism. The Cathedral of Chartres and the Abbey of Mont-Saint-Michel, so greatly admired by Henry Adams, were not 'made possible' by the institutions of capitalism. True, ours is a very different social structure from those under which Plato and Saint Thomas lived, and we have no intention of returning to the ways of life of the thirteenth century A.D. or the fourth century B.C. But these analogies at least raise the question whether a civilization of some sort might not also be achieved without benefit of capitalism in the twenty-first century A.D., or even in the twentieth.

The pattern of capitalism is not engraved upon the foundations of organized society. It is only the frosting of the social cake, the latest and topmost cultural deposit, and the one which is therefore most accessible and most susceptible to revision with the least disturbance to all that lies below.

To change the figure again, the situation is that of a pile of blocks. The topmost block is out of balance and needs to be shifted or replaced. If that is not done, to be sure, the disequilibrium of the top block may bring down the entire pile. It is also true that, since the top block rests on each lower block down to the very bottom, an upheaval at the bottom will displace the ailing top and very likely the entire pile. But, as even the smallest child can see, shifting the bottom blocks is no way to restore the balance at the top. That is not what the situation calls for, although it may conceivably happen.

The alternative to capitalism is already plainly visible. The alternative to non-consumption is consumption. Even the American people, with the highest standards of living the world has ever known, could eat vastly more food, wear more and better clothes, occupy more and better houses, drive more automobiles, fly more airplanes, go to more schools, read more books, listen to more music, look at more pictures, and as a result of it all think better thoughts and form higher ideals than ever before.

No one has ever doubted this. On the contrary, it is an ancient dogma of economic orthodoxy that wants are infinite. Nor is there any question about the productive potency of the industrial economy. A careful statistical study made ten years ago by a leading research organization showed that full use of the equipment and manpower existing and available in 1929 would have been sufficient to raise the consumption of every family in the United States to the equivalent of twenty-five hundred dollars (in 1929 dollars) without any reduction at any other point. Another study of 'the potential product capacity' of American industry set a very much higher figure, one so high as to provoke considerable skepticism among more conservative economists. Yet in view of the present volume of war production such doubts now seem a little academic.

This does not mean that the entire population of the world, or even of America, could recline forthwith in the lap of luxury. Economists who feel an aversion to the whole idea of 'an economy of abundance' for other reasons still point sternly at the hole in the economic doughnut. To achieve 'full' production the community would have to work. Greater production would exhaust resources faster. With all Americans raised to the level of twenty-five hundred dollars a year, vast hordes in other countries would still be on the edge of starvation.

But all calculations such as these are beside the point. The issue which capitalism raises is not that of the ultimate attainable utopia. What is at issue is our present failure to consume what is in fact currently produced, the failure which causes the product of current production to be stored in warehouses or dumped on the foreign market. It can scarcely be denied that the alternative to storing and dumping is consuming.

Why do we fail to consume? Obviously because as a community we lack the means to buy. The real problem is not that of consumption as such, but that of the distribution of income upon which all consumption is contingent. That is the real trouble spot, the major source of economic distress throughout modern times.

What the present economic situation calls for is a re-
dressing of the present flow of income such as will effect a
sufficient flow of mass-consumer purchasing power to absorb
the present actual product of industry. Only that. No
utopia can be expected to follow such a change. If the
change is made directly and with the greatest economy of
means according to the best engineering practice, great
extremes of wealth and (relative) poverty will still exist.
Great injustices will still obtain. The New Jerusalem will
still seem to be as far away as ever, for infinity is somewhat
remote by definition quite irrespective of finite change.
Plenty of scope for idealism will still remain.

But for whatever it may be worth industrial society will
have been saved. All that is necessary to do is to redress
very slightly the present flow of income. That need not involve any modification of the foundations of Western society, let alone all society. Moreover, it is perfectly obvious
what the top block is. We have no excuse of ignorance. But
time is running out. The whole pile is increasingly unsteady.
The top block must be identified and moved at once.

11

The Great Divide

According to the books the entire income of the community is divided among the 'factors of production' in the form of wages, rent, interest, and profits. How this is done forms an important part of the legend of capitalism. The legend is that each 'factor' receives exactly what it deserves. The laborer, the landlord, the moneylender, and the manipulating financier — each is worthy of his hire.

For the present crisis, however, this formula is not particularly significant, for two reasons.

For one thing, the legend is pretty threadbare at this point. Many critics have long since pointed out the obvious defects of this theory of distribution. The whole thing is simply a tautology. We call these agents 'factors of production,' but in actuality we identify them, not in terms of what they do, but in terms of the income they receive. Thus, the laborer is not identified by his sweat. Housewives do not qualify as laborers however hard they work. A laborer is one who works for wages. We then go on to declare that the income received by laborers (that is, those who receive wages) is wages.

The argument by which we establish that the wages are

just is somewhat more complicated, but it comes down to this. If we know what wages labor is getting, and if we assume the impossibility of labor's getting any more — conditions being what they are — then it appears that labor is getting all it can, conditions being what they are. Each factor receives exactly what it produces, if you mean by 'what it produces' what it receives.

But there is a second and more important reason for ignoring the wages, rent, interest, and profits of labor, land, capital, and management in the present crisis. What is important in the present situation is not the name of a person's income, but its amount. The significant thing is that some incomes are small and some are large. Many are small and only a few are very large. If we adopt twenty-five hundred dollars as our base (since this is the point to which the Brookings Institution showed that every family in the country might have been raised by full production in 1929), and if we apply this yardstick to the income pattern of the year 1936 (the only year in which a nation-wide survey of consumer incomes has ever been made), then we discover that in this year 87.43 per cent of all the families in the United States received family incomes lower than our basic twenty-five hundred dollars.

This state of affairs did not originate with capitalism. If we look at it in the large, as Disraeli did in the much-quoted remark that the King of England rules over two separate and distinct kingdoms, the rich and the poor, we know that this condition is a very ancient one. 'The poor ye have always with you' was said nearly two thousand years ago. The feudal order which preceded capitalism likewise divided the community into many who were poor and a few who were (relatively) rich.

Consequently, it goes without saying that the discrepancy between riches and poverty is very deeply embedded in the institutions of organized society. It goes clear to the bottom of the pile of blocks. In a certain sense the institutions of capitalism do no more than preserve feudal distinctions, giving them slightly different forms characteristic of the age of industry.

Nevertheless, the discrepancy between small incomes and large incomes is very significant in our present situation, for two reasons.

In the first place, as we have already noted, the differential between small incomes and large incomes corresponds exactly with the differential between small savings (or none at all) and large savings. The larger the income, the greater is the *proportion* of it that is saved. Hence it follows that if our economy is suffering from oversaving and underconsumption (and we know it is), the point at which the damage is done is the point at which the community income is divided so as to flow into many little channels and a few big ones. The trouble may be very deepseated. But what is wrong can be stated very simply. Small incomes are too small and big ones are too big — too small to consume the product of industry and too big for investment in a market so limited.

In the second place, this trouble is progressive. As the community income increases in periods of prosperity and industrial expansion, the part of it that flows into large incomes cuts ever deeper and wider channels. This tendency is a matter of fact. Statistical studies have revealed it clearly. For example, during the nineteen-twenties wages were going up, and the total receipts of labor were going up, though not as fast as individual wage rates; but the receipts of labor were not increasing as fast as the national income. This was the 'New Era' of high-wage prosperity. The poor were getting richer. But the irony of the situation lay in the fact that the rich were getting richer faster. The poor were getting richer only as measured by their former poverty; measured by present riches they were getting steadily poorer. The increase of mass-consumer purchasing power was not keeping pace with the expansion of industry, so that it was only a matter of time until the community was brought up with a jolt to the realization that provision had been made for a volume of goods which could not possibly be sold.

This disposition of large incomes to increase faster than small ones, like the basic discrepancy between riches and poverty, is very deeply embedded in the social structure. The institutions which determine the condition of the masses are essentially static. It is easier for a few individuals to change their way of life than for a whole community to do so. The basic motivation of capitalism may appeal to the whole community; but the appeal is to individual self-aggrandizement, not to community betterment.

In addition to all this, certain specific features of our economy seem to contribute to the trend. One is technological unemployment. Another is the differential movement of prices.

Periods of expanding industry are always periods of technological improvement. Obviously anyone who is setting up a new plant will not try to duplicate the machinery of obsolete design with which many old plants are still operating. He will install only machinery of latest design. This process would, therefore, increase the preponderance of new machinery in the industry even if no new inventions were to appear. But new inventions do appear, and do find the chance to be tried out in a period of expansion.

All these improvements of design economize labor as well as weight, horsepower, materials, and so on. Fewer workers are required to produce a given unit of product. Some of them may have to be highly skilled. Their individual wages may be considerably higher than the old average. That is why individual wage-scales are an unreliable index. But reduction in number of workers may, and usually does, mean that the labor-cost per unit of product is reduced. That is, the flow of income to small incomes is reduced relatively to the total flow of income.

Meantime the whole price-level may be going up. This is likely to be the case in a period of expansion. But, as everybody knows, prices are not all equally sensitive. Some move faster than others. The prices of basic commodities, such as are dealt with on the floors of commodity exchanges and boards of trade, vary from hour to hour. This is true, for example, of cotton. Basic manufactured goods, such as cloth in the bolt, vary faster than even the wholesale prices of finished goods, such as overalls and dresses; and wholesale prices are more sensitive than retail prices.

Wages are at the tail-end of this series. For workers only feel the pinch when retail prices have registered a perceptible general rise, or when general business expansion has reached such a pitch as to take up all the slack of the 'industrial reserve army' of the unemployed and even to create a scarcity of certain classes of workers. In unionized industries wage contracts often run for specified periods, such as a year, regardless of price movements in the meantime.

This disposition of wages to trail in a rising market still further accentuates the discrepancy between the mass of small incomes and the larger incomes. The analysis could be extended to the circumstances affecting farm incomes and

many other aspects of the economy; and what it all adds up
to is a pronounced and stubborn trend. As the community
income expands, the proportion of it which flows into small
incomes steadily diminishes.

This is the condition which capitalism has glorified with
its legend of the creative function of capital (fund) accumulation, and this is the condition which has doomed the
capitalistic economy to recurrent depression and to perennial economic warfare. This is what has to be corrected if
the final doom of total revolution is to be averted.

12

Full Employment

THE TEST of an adequate flow of consumer purchasing power through the mass of small incomes is full employment. That is what we mean by full employment, and that is all we mean by it.

Obviously there is no such thing as absolutely full employment except universal slavery; that is, involuntary employment. Voluntary full employment can mean only one thing: the availability of jobs to all who seek them. As Sir William Beveridge points out, this means a state of affairs in which jobs are seeking men rather than the other way about; that is, a seller's market for labor.

This condition justifies itself on humanitarian grounds. Beveridge himself makes full use of this appeal. 'A person,' he says, 'who has difficulty in buying the labor that he wants suffers inconvenience or reduction of profits. A person who cannot sell his labor is in effect told that he is of no use. The first difficulty causes annoyance or loss. The other is a personal catastrophe.' He even goes so far as to say that 'The human difference between failing to buy and failing to sell labor is the decisive reason for aiming to make the labor market a seller's rather than a buyer's market.'

Even so, the decisive consideration is the flow of income.

When we deplore unemployment, it is not the idleness we deplore, but the destitution. For the overwhelming majority — say ninety-nine per cent — of the people, employment means receipt of income; and unemployment means loss of the chief source — for most people the only source — of income. Such loss is indeed a personal calamity. But this calamity is obviously greater the greater is the number of people who suffer it. If it could be demonstrated that only by leaving one person in a hundred unemployed could the other ninety-nine retain their employment; that forcing the hundredth person on some employer would make the difference between solvency and bankruptcy and so would throw the entire hundred out of work; then a strong case would be made for letting the hundredth worker languish.

This is precisely what capitalism has argued in the past. It is true, as Sir William Beveridge declares, that 'The labor market in the past has invariably, or all but invariably, been a buyer's market rather than a seller's market, with more unemployed men — generally many more unemployed men — than unfilled jobs.' The perennially unemployed thus filled the ranks of what Marx called 'the industrial reserve army' on which employers have always been able to draw to break strikes and to prevent a labor shortage from raising wages.

Marx's ironies seem to imply a deliberate conspiracy. But in fact employers, like the community at large, have been moved by faith, a touchingly naïve faith, that the laws of nature, in particular Say's law of markets, would keep men and jobs in equilibrium. What has betrayed our innocence has been the differential flow of income. With income continually flowing faster into large-income channels where funds are accumulated for investment than into small-income channels through which mass-consumer purchasing power flows, the purchasing power of the ninety-and-nine has been insufficient to sustain their own continued employment. The poor wretch who was sacrificed in their behalf was sacrificed in vain.

Unemployment is a menace because it is epidemic. Any unemployment at all means a constriction of the flow of mass-consumer purchasing power by which alone all employment is sustained. A policy of full employment is a good policy because full employment means the maximum possible flow of mass-consumer purchasing power. For full employment also is epidemic. Since it is the flow of mass-consumer purchasing power that sustains employment, and since the incomes of the employed themselves determine the volume of that current, increasing employment means increasing the ability of the economy to sustain employment.

How can this be done? Since it is the differential flow of income that is the cause of all the trouble, it is likewise the differential flow of income that provides the cure. The causes of that differential are deepseated and various. To achieve perfection it would be necessary to root out all those causes. But fortunately correction of the flow of income need not await that far-off divine event. Regardless of what causes income to flow faster in large-income channels than in small-income channels, we can say with certainty that anything which reverses this differential is to the good. Whatever reduces the flow of income to large incomes will help sustain full employment, and whatever increases the flow of income to small incomes will help sustain full employment.

This is true of all measures, irrespective of their other features. But obviously some measures affect the flow of income more directly and economically than others. The question is, What measures affect the flow of income most directly and with least incidental disturbance of the prevailing social structure?

13

Abolish Property?

THE INSTITUTION OF PROPERTY has more effect on the flow
of income than any other institution. Indeed, we might
even define property as that institution by which the flow
of income is determined. Consequently, any substantial
modification of this institution will have a correspondingly
substantial effect on the flow of income.

It will also have many other effects which may or may not
be desirable in any given circumstances. Property is one of
the basic institutions of all organized society, one of the
blocks at the very bottom of the pile. Like other basic institutions it is a complex bundle of rights and obligations,
traditions, attitudes, and social practices of the widest possible variety. These are all closely interwoven with the practices, attitudes, and rights that go to make up the other
basic institutions, all of which have been differentiated over
an immense span of time from primitive culture complexes
in which considerations of property were virtually indistin-
guishable from the patterns of political life, family life, and
even religious life. Consequently, any substantial change in
the pattern of property is bound to affect all the other institutions in greater or less degree.

All this has to be taken into account. Granted that a change in the flow of income is necessary and that a major operation on the institution of property will effect such a change, we still have two important questions to answer. Is such an operation necessary? And is it desirable?

Like other basic institutions, the property complex is continually undergoing change. Such changes have been especially pronounced in modern times as a consequence of the industrial revolution. Scholars are generally agreed that the institution of property has undergone a major change within the last century.

As it exists today the institution of property seems to perform two major functions, those of income and management. For many years these two functions have been splitting apart. They have not become entirely separated and it is doubtful if they ever can be. Nevertheless, the differentiation is already quite extreme.

As this institution emerged from feudalism, its meaning was focused upon the physical properties over which the owner exercised control and from which he derived an income. But in the course of the intervening centuries, and especially during the last century or so, the growth of the corporation has resulted in the funding of the bulk of the productive wealth of the community, with the result that ownership no longer has direct reference to any particular bit of physical property, but rather constitutes a claim upon a specified share of the earnings of the corporation. Meantime control has become similarly diffuse. Notoriously the men who control the affairs of great systems of interlocking corporations hardly ever own more than a minute fraction of the properties they control, while the owners of great fortunes often have no share in the control — assume no responsibility whatever for the conduct — of the businesses from which their incomes are derived.

Economists are virtually unanimous in their agreement that this change is indeed momentous. The existence of property and its importance in our economy have not changed. The institution for which our Constitution set up its most elaborate safeguards is still sacred. But the pattern has changed. Property has become in effect two institutions: an income institution and a control institution.

Having a more or less independent existence, each of these institutions is subject to more or less independent modification. Each is subject to more or less distinct governmental regulation. This is well illustrated in the case of income by the personal income tax. Two individuals may both own shares in the same corporation which might conceivably be the only source of income for both recipients. Nevertheless, the taxes they pay, and the residual incomes they are permitted to retain, may be different, not only in amount, but even in rate, since each is determined, not by the nature of the physical property owned, but by the amount of the recipient's net taxable income. The same is true in the case of control. Thus, the operation of a bank or a public utility company is subject to various federal and state regulations quite irrespective of the division of its earnings.

This fact provides a clear and decisive answer to one of our two questions. It means that income patterns can be modified quite independently of the control patterns. Liquidation of private property in the instruments of production will transform both. But that is not the only way the flow of income can be dealt with. The separation of the income function from the control function means that income patterns are subject to modification — even total transformation

— by measures which leave the operation of industry virtually unaffected.

Is this desirable? Certainly it is not desirable that the operation of industry should be subject to no regulation whatever. Everybody now agrees, for example, that pure food and drug regulation is desirable. We agree also that some industries should be publicly owned and operated. This is true, for example, of the building, maintenance, and operation of highways. It may well be that some industries which are still private have come to be so largely 'affected with the public interest' that they also should be publicly owned and operated. A modicum of regulation may have to be extended to many industries which are now largely unregulated, perhaps at certain points to all. Many businessmen now advocate uniform incorporation laws or even federal incorporation.

Nevertheless, sudden and sweeping change, such as the 'nationalization' of all industry, or even of all basic industries, may be highly undesirable. Quite apart from the general social disintegration which would inevitably result from the liquidation of any major institution, the operation of industry is now an extremely formidable affair in all advanced industrial communities. In such communities management is a highly specialized function. To be sure, a great deal of what is grandly designated as managerial skill is skill in the arts of banditry which, however profitable it may be to its practitioners, is in no sense an asset to the community. But there still remains a considerable body of knowledge and experience, together with a vast organization, that is a community asset. All this would be jeopardized by sudden and complete liquidation.

If all the executives were to walk out of a given business

taking with them all their professional assistants, together with all their files and records, and turning the whole plant over to somebody else to run, the successor would have a hard time. At the outset he would not know even where to turn for raw materials or for buyers of his product. All those things can be learned, but learning takes time; in particular, the creation of a competent organization takes time; and in the meantime disorder would prevail. For the economy as a whole the disorder would be considerable. In advanced industrial countries it could easily be fatal. General starvation might ensue. Recent experience of military governments in liberated countries is highly indicative, though in these cases the military governments enjoy the great advantage of being able to draw on the going economies of their home countries.

The indications are that advanced industrial countries would be well advised to avoid sudden and sweeping change in the organization and control of industry. The case of Russia is no precedent. For it must never be forgotten that Russia was the least industrialized country of Europe, far less industrialized in 1917 than now. What happened in Russia in 1917 and the years immediately following was disconcerting enough, but it gives scarcely a hint of what might happen if the United States were to try a similar experiment.

Fortunately we are under no such necessity. The flow of income is susceptible to modification quite independently of the operational pattern of industry. One revolution at a time! When the crisis of capitalism has been averted, there will then be time enough for a systematic and progressive attack on the problem of industrial organization.

14

Can Private Business Do It?

Under the private ownership of industry by far the greater part of employment is likewise private. This means that private employers seem to have it in their power to maintain full employment such as would provide a flow of mass-consumer purchasing power adequate to absorb the output of industry at full production.

Private employers themselves say they can and will do this. Indeed, their loud protestations echo throughout the land. To be sure, some critics dismiss these avowals as organized propaganda having no other meaning or intent except to head off the governmental actions which would be the inevitable alternative to private initiative. But it is neither necessary nor possible to question the sincerity of the spokesmen of private business. Sincerity is a matter of personal sentiment — and how can individual sentiment be measured? No doubt the sentiments of businessmen are as mixed as those of all the rest of us. But what matters is not the attitudes of businessmen as individuals, but the grounds on which they make their claims and their power to deliver what they promise.

What reason have we to suppose that private business can achieve full employment by its own efforts? Can it do so in fact? Obviously our past experience is one of failure. Private business has not succeeded in maintaining full employment in the past. Have conditions changed in any significant respect?

Certainly no new reason has been advanced in recent years for supposing that private business can now succeed where it has failed before. On the contrary, the sole ground on which this claim is made today is that of orthodox capitalism. The idea is that capital funds alone give employment. Presumably the very existence of a sum of money is sufficient to insure industrial activity, provided only the money is left in private hands, is not diminished by taxation or subjected to any regulation such as might diminish profits, incentives, etc., etc. Apparently if all the money there is were only removed from the squandering hands of the mass of consumers and placed in the enlightened custody of businessmen, full employment would ensue forthwith.

Mentality such as this, however sincere, affords no basis for further confidence, and there has been only one significant change. Some business leaders do seem to recognize today that business as usual will not suffice. They admit that things have not gone as well as could be desired in the past. They even admit that leaving things to private initiative will not suffice, that businessmen must get together and make a concerted effort to maintain full employment. In part this seems to mean only an exercise of will power, as though disaster could be averted by a sort of economic faith-healing. In part, however, and on the part of some of the more enlightened business leaders, this determination does constitute an admission of past fault. It is admitted that the flow of income has gone awry. Prices have been too high and wages have been too low. What is, therefore, proposed is a concerted effort on the part of businessmen to keep prices down and wages up.

If it could be done, this would indeed do the trick. There is no question but that generally lower prices (in relation to a given flow of purchasing power) and higher wages (in the sense of an increased total flow of income through wage channels) would indeed redress the differential flow of income. If carried far enough, it would sustain continuous full employment and save the capitalist system. But is it possible? Is it compatible with the actualities of capitalism?

By definition capitalism is a régime of private moneymaking, and moneymaking is a matter of buying cheap and selling dear. For any individual businessman to sell for less than he can get, or to pay his labor more than other people pay, is to invite bankruptcy. Under competition it is to insure bankruptcy, for under competition the presumption is that prices continually hover at the point at which they barely cover the cost of production, and wages at the point at which they barely suffice to attract enough labor to produce just the amount of goods that can be sold at going prices. For businessmen to promise to market goods at lower prices than that, or to pay labor higher wages than that, is to promise what no businessman can possibly deliver under competition, since the attempt to do so would promptly eliminate him from the ranks of solvent businessmen.

Either such a promise is an empty gesture — so empty as to invite suspicion of its sincerity — or it refers to other than competitive conditions. In fact the latter is actually the case. The business spokesmen who earnestly advocate lower prices and higher wages in order to achieve full employment through private initiative are quite frank in admitting the prevalence of monopoly. They admit it, and they deplore it, and they propose to abate it.

Can they deliver what they promise? This question raises an interesting paradox. Monopoly exists when (and to the extent that) businessmen act in concert to maintain higher prices for what they sell or lower prices for what they buy (including labor) than would prevail under competition. If the effect of competition is to bring prices into close relation to cost of production, the effect of monopoly is to bring selling prices above, or buying prices below, that point. Such prices, therefore, offer a margin within the limits of which an individual businessman conceivably might reduce his prices, or raise wages, and still keep afloat. But in doing so he would be bucking the monopoly. And since the monopoly represents a group of businessmen whose concerted power is sufficient to prevent that sort of thing, it goes without saying that such an individual businessman would be prevented forthwith by all the very interesting means which monopolies employ in dealing with such cases.

In this case also the individual businessman is powerless. But this is clearly recognized by the reformers, who therefore propose joint action. What is proposed is that businessmen should act in concert to prevent themselves from acting in concert. That is, they should do good in concert where previously they have done evil in concert.

Strangely enough, this is by no means impossible. But it is not capitalism in the familiar and historic sense. On the contrary, it represents the almost total abandonment of the ideas and policies of absolute capitalism. That is what is most significant about the present general acceptance of the principle of full employment. That principle is directly contradictory of the basic dogma of capitalism. Whether businessmen realize it or not — and while some seem to do so, others certainly do not — in committing themselves to a policy of full employment they are abandoning absolute capitalism.

They are also nullifying one of the dogmas of revolutionary theory, namely, that no ruling class ever voluntarily relinquishes its power. Indeed, this may be the key to the whole situation. It may be true that a ruling class never commits suicide, but history is full of instances in which the powers and functions of a ruling class have undergone more or less voluntary transformation. The British crown experienced such a change without ceasing to exist, and did so with the acquiescence of a long series of individual kings. The British aristocracy allowed itself to be absorbed into the capitalist class, and vice versa.

It is by no means impossible that men of wealth might be sufficiently enlightened and realistic to acquiesce in a modification of their rôle, seeing perhaps that total liquidation is the sole possible alternative. For many years businessmen have been talking the gospel of service, and it may turn out that what has been only empty talk hitherto has nevertheless prepared its votaries for the reality. It would not be the first time a propagandist has ended by convincing himself.

There is another paradox in the proposal of businessmen to act in concert to achieve full employment. They propose to do so in order to forestall government regulation and even ownership. But government is a function, not a distinct entity. Government is the activity in which men engage and the agency through which they act when they act in concert. Monopoly itself is a trend away from private enterprise and toward quasi-governmental function. It was Marx himself who expected government ownership to germinate from monopoly. Concerted action on the part of businessmen in the public interest — that is, to make the economy work by maintaining continuous full employment — would be more-than-quasi governmental. If the United States Chamber of Commerce were to become the agency through which such a policy were realized, that achievement would make the Chamber itself an agency of government.

There is nothing objectionable about this. On the contrary, it is a consummation devoutly to be wished. Probably it is the only solution of the monopoly problem alternative to total liquidation of private business. That is, either business must become public through its own germinative processes or it will suffer extinction. But these are slow processes, and the crisis of capitalism brooks no delay. We cannot wait to see whether private business may have the intelligence and vitality to socialize itself. If time is to be afforded for such a process, the flow of income must be rectified at once. The business leaders who promise full employment show no inclination to post any bond for the fulfillment of their promise, and we must have immediate delivery. However significant such promises may be, promises are not enough. Immediate action is required, and to be immediate the action must be far more specific than anything our present business leaders have in mind.

15

The Magic of the Interest Rate

ALL INDUSTRY GIVES EMPLOYMENT, and all employment swells the flow of mass-consumer purchasing power through wage channels. But one form of industry is especially important in these respects.

This form of industry is sometimes known as 'capital goods' industry, because its products are not used by consumers to 'satisfy their wants,' but are used by producers as tools, equipment, plant, or raw materials of further production. It is also sometimes known as 'durable goods' industry, because its products for the most part are not used up immediately as food and clothes are used up, but enjoy a considerable span of life as buildings and machinery do. In the present discussion, however, this type of industry will be identified as 'construction goods' industry, because that phrase points more directly than any other at the particular characteristic of that industry with which the present discussion is concerned.

Construction goods industries are 'feast-or-famine' industries. That is, to an appalling degree they tend either to run full blast or to close down altogether. The reason for this is quite apparent. Take a clear-cut case such as a locomotive works, clear-cut because the product, locomotives, is something that nobody uses except railways and they only for the purpose of hauling trains. If railways, who are the sole consumers of locomotives, bought them the way most of us buy bread and milk, a loaf or a bottle a day, rain or shine, in good times and bad times very much the same, since we have to eat in adversity as well as in prosperity, and these are the basic foods we can scarcely do without, there would be no story. The point is that railways are very different from people and locomotives are very different from bread and milk.

Railways buy locomotives only when their traffic is increasing. In a depression, when traffic is decreasing, locomotives do not wear out as fast as when traffic is heavier. But most important is the fact that in a depression with revenues dwindling railways are financially unable to afford new locomotives. Consequently they do without, patch up the old ones and make them run a little farther, and postpone replacement until better times.

But good times and bad times are general conditions. Consequently all railways do without together, and all railways order replacements and additions together. This means that locomotive builders are sometimes swamped with orders, and sometimes have no business at all, as general business conditions improve or worsen.

This feast-or-famine behavior of the construction industries has a terrible impact on the whole economy, especially through the fluctuation of employment. For all the many employees of these industries are also consumers. A considerable stream of consumer purchasing power flows through their pay envelopes. When business conditions are improving and railways, seeing the prospect of more revenues and the need to haul more trains, all at once order more locomotives, the locomotive builders take on thousands of employees. These employees, who have been in a state of economic suspended animation perhaps for years, begin to buy their children imperatively needed clothes and start thinking about a washing machine, or even a new house; and all this flood of consumer purchasing power still further stimulates the market. It even makes more traffic for the railways and increases their impatience for new locomotives. Likewise, when the employees of locomotive builders are laid off, they stop buying all these things, and this still further deepens the depression, even drying up railway traffic and closing down locomotives works tighter than ever.

This cumulative effect of employment or unemployment is known to economists as 'the multiplier.' It operates throughout all industry. Every increase or decrease of employment means a corresponding increase or decrease in the flow of consumer purchasing power which in turn means a corresponding increase or decrease of production generally.

College towns offer a very pretty example of this principle. Population figures seem to show that the 'civilian' population of college towns is just about three times the college enrollment. A college with an enrollment of a thousand ordinarily supports a town with a population of three thousand. When college enrollment goes to fifteen hundred, the town grows to forty-five hundred. When it falls to seven hundred, the town dwindles to twenty-one hundred. Not all of these townspeople are gainfully employed, of course. Of the total number of men, women, children, the very old, the sick and disabled, infants, the idle rich, probably not more than a third are breadwinners. This means that for every person 'employed' as a college student, one other is employed in a 'civilian' capacity. The multiplier has a value of two.

Some such effect as this runs through all business. But it is especially pronounced in the case of the construction industries. Indeed, the spasmodic behavior of these industries is so pronounced, and its effect on the flow of mass-consumer purchasing power is so important, as to raise the question whether the whole problem may not center at this point. If only the construction industries could be made to operate continuously — at a constant rate of gradual expansion corresponding to the rate of continuous expansion of the whole economy — then, surely, the problem would be solved. The question is, How can the construction industries be induced to follow such a course?

For several reasons the interest rate seems to offer a tempting solution of the problem. It makes an immediate appeal both to businessmen and to economists. It is itself a 'business proposition.' At the same time it works in its mysterious ways its wonders to perform. For several generations economists have been even more susceptible than businessmen to the fascination of the subtle and automatic adjustments of the all-pervading price system, and any agency which operates in this fashion through this system is therefore blessed in advance with a measure of plausibility. Moreover, there are specific situations in which the interest rate does seem to be the decisive factor in critically important business decisions.

Everyone is familiar with the case of the man who has an idea for setting himself up in business. Opportunity is knocking at his door. If only he could take advantage of his chance, the business he would create would give employment and would therefore contribute its multiplying effect to general prosperity. But he 'lacks capital' — that is, capital funds. He might perhaps borrow the necessary funds. But at this point the interest rate appears to be the crucial consideration. A high rate of interest may impose such a burden on the prospective business as to be prohibitory at the outset. In such a case a lower rate of interest seems to make the difference between business expansion and stagnation.

The same thing seems to be true when this situation is viewed from the other side. By definition, all savings (that is, funds accumulated for investment) seek investment. In so far as they find it, they flow into the market as purchasing power to absorb the product of industry. They absorb producers' goods (or construction goods, or capital goods) precisely as consumer purchasing power absorbs consumers' goods. The two channels supplement each other. Together they constitute the total market for the product of industry.

Furthermore, it is in the savings-investment channel that the clogging occurs which is so fatally multiplied by the behavior of the construction goods industries. Owing to the differential flow of income — the tendency for income to flow faster into large incomes, where saving occurs, than into small ones — the current of savings constantly threatens to burst its banks. How can this turbulent flow be conducted safely through the channels of investment to the market for producers' (construction) goods? How can people who have money to invest find the 'investment opportunities' which they require?

From this point of view also the answer seems to be, By offering their funds at bargain rates. The presumption is that a lower rate of interest would induce businessmen like the one described above to borrow more money and put it into more industrial plant.

Economists have buttressed this idea with a great variety of subtle theoretical arguments, all of which, however, spring from the mythological potency of capital. This is true even of the argument of the late J. M. Keynes (Lord Keynes). No one has done more than he to make other economists see the fatal hiatus between saving and invest-ment and the chronic underemployment and deficiency of purchasing power from which the capitalist economy suf-fers, and no other economist has shown more courage in fac-ing the necessity of breaking with absolute capitalism. He was even prepared to face the disappearance of all income from invested capital. But he expected this to come about as a result of the interest rate gradually falling until it reaches zero, and he expected this to result from the increasing pro-fusion of capital.

But what is meant by 'capital' in such an argument is never altogether clear. Is this capital the physical equip-ment of industry? In this case, obviously, there can never be too much. More physical plant means more industry and a higher level of consumption for the whole community, not the progressive worthlessness of physical plant. Or does 'capital' refer in this argument to capital funds? But in that case why should we suppose that a surfeit of capital funds will bring the interest rate down to zero and so break the hold of capital-fund-owners on the economy? It never has, though surfeit of funds has been a recurrent condition throughout modern times. That is precisely the condition, or one aspect of the condition, we are trying to correct.

The truth is, of course, that the interest rate is not the 'sufficient cause' of these disorders. What prevents the in-dividual businessman from obtaining funds to embark on a promising venture — assuming that its promise is real and demonstrable, and that the businessman is trustworthy — is a general condition of business recession in which considerable doubt exists whether any venture, however promising in itself, will find enough customers to make it go. The real obstacle, if one exists outside the venture itself, is the deficiency of mass-consumer purchasing power. If purchasing power is running strong, the difference of a small per cent in the interest rate will make no difference; if the stream of purchasing power is sluggish, the venture would be a bad risk at zero rate of interest.

The same is true of the economy as a whole. What slows down the economy is not the hiatus between saving and investment, but rather the fact that a surfeit of saving inevitably means a deficiency of mass-consumer purchasing power, and this means a dwindling market for the consumers' goods in which all industrial activity eventuates. When such a deficiency exists, not even the investment of the total flow of savings at an interest rate approaching zero would bring full recovery. While the investment process was going on, the construction industries would indeed be restored to life and the wages of their employees would indeed flow through consuming channels. In that case the basic deficiency of consumer purchasing power would not be multiplied, as it ordinarily is, by the stagnation of the construction industries. But so long as the differential flow of income persisted, in consequence of which saving originally threatened to exceed investment, the basic deficiency of mass-consumer purchasing power would likewise persist; and in spite of the employment of workers in the construction industries, it would eventually mean that plant was being provided for a larger volume of product than could be absorbed by the basically deficient flow of mass-consumer purchasing power.

This does not mean that high interest rates are to be preferred. Quite apart from this argument, lower interest rates are desirable for a variety of reasons. If Keynes could have got his 'rentier class' to commit suicide by reducing the interest rate to zero, that eventuality would be quite acceptable to most of us. In the meantime, lower rates of interest contribute their mite directly to the increased flow of consumer purchasing power.

For consumers also borrow money. Lower rates of interest on automobile liens and house mortgages mean lower rents and cheaper cars, and this means more houses built and more cars bought, which means more production and more general prosperity. Highly significant in this regard is the success of the Federal Housing Authority in stimulating house construction by making lower interest rates available to householders.

Certain classes of producers also are prevented by various special considerations from having access to money markets at reasonable rates. It has been demonstrated that farm loans at low rates of interest pay off in a big way, and there is considerable evidence that the same may be true of small business generally.

But none of these considerations is decisive for the economy as a whole. If the test of all these measures is their ability to swell the flow of mass-consumer purchasing power, then reduction of interest on loans to consumers, though desirable as far as it goes, is of relatively slight importance. And that is the test. As a general solvent, the interest rate is quite inadequate. Though it would affect the multiplier, it would not alter the basic condition which the multiplier only multiplies and does not create. What creates it is the differential flow of income. The solution of the problem can be found only in the correction of that differential.

16

The Rôle of Public Works

GOVERNMENT can induce a flow of consumer purchasing power sufficient to absorb the entire product of industry, however large the volume of production may be. This is what actually happens in wartime. Hence the familiar lament that we should be able to nerve ourselves to take the steps which are necessary to bring our economy to the highest peak of efficiency only under the lash of war.

In this respect war is quite literally a gigantic system of public works. Obviously war has other aspects of a less attractive character. But public works as such do not necessarily involve death and destruction. Government projects are not limited to the production of munitions of war. On the contrary, a public works program may produce monuments of enduring value. The Public Works Administration did so during the nineteen-thirties, as everybody knows. Consequently public works have come to be accepted almost universally as by far the most desirable of governmental recovery measures.

There can be no doubt that public works programs are here to stay, and this is altogether to the good. The question is whether public works are sufficiently potent by themselves to bear the entire responsibility of maintaining the balance of the economy.

Public works increase the flow of consumer purchasing power in two distinct ways. First and most obviously, they give employment. This is a source of great satisfaction to all those, poor as well as rich, whose Puritan-capitalist consciences are offended by anything resembling charity. In one respect, indeed, this satisfaction is entirely justified. Since people employed on public works are indeed employees in the same sense as people who are employed on private works, there is no reason why they should not be paid salaries and wages comparable to those received by people who perform comparable functions in private industry. Architects, engineers, plumbers, electricians, structural steel workers, stonemasons, and all the rest are, and properly should be, paid as such when they are employed on public works projects no less than when they are employed in private industry. None of them is 'on relief.' Consequently the flow of consumer purchasing power through their aggregate pay envelopes is considerably larger than would be true of the same number of relief clients, and this is countenanced by public conscience in view of their respectability as employees.

In addition to this direct flow of consumer purchasing power we must also take account of the public works themselves. Mr. Winthrop Aldrich once undertook to prove that all public works are liabilities and not assets, since they saddle the community with the cost of their perpetual maintenance and do not, for the most part, bring in any income. This would mean, apparently, that whereas a private tollbridge is an asset the same bridge would be a liability if it were built with public funds and opened to public use without charge. What Mr. Aldrich overlooked in this interesting argument is the value of the bridge to the public that uses it. If the use of the bridge on a toll basis is worth ten cents a head, the value of the free bridge to the community is the same as though a public functionary were to stand at one end of the bridge and present every traveler with a dime which another functionary then collected at the other end.

All public works make a direct contribution to the standard of living (or level of consumption) of the community which uses them. To the extent provided by the works in question the community's consumption is enlarged. This is true whether the public work is a park, a swimming pool, a courthouse, a university library, a slum-clearance housing project, or an electric power development. All these undertakings give employment, absorb the product of industry, and raise the level of community living.

But if all these things are consumed on a community basis, they are also paid for on a community basis. A public bridge differs from a tollbridge just as a public school differs from a private school. In each case the public work is paid for by the citizens, whether as individuals they use it or not. This means that the decision to embark on such an undertaking is made by public officials and not by private businessmen, and it is made on the basis of judgment of public need and not on the basis of prospective profits. This does not mean that one type of judgment is necessarily any more fallible than the other. To take an extreme case, a gambling casino may hold out the prospect of very considerable profits; but the representatives of the community may nevertheless decide with considerable assurance that what the community needs is a school. At the same time it is quite apparent that the more extensive such a program of public works becomes, the more carefully it must be planned. That is why there is so much anxious insistence on planning now for the works programs which may be necessary to take up the slack in the postwar years.

Particularly delicate is the relation between public works and private industry. Within limits, and notwithstanding the arguments of Mr. Winthrop Aldrich, businessmen generally favor public works. They do so for this special reason in addition to the considerations recited above. The typical public work is by definition a building project. As such it is a consumer of building materials and of construction goods generally. This means that public works projects act as a restorative to the construction goods industries.

This is an important consideration which nevertheless carries an equally important limitation. Enthusiasm for public works is by no means confined to those who have a financial stake in the construction goods industries. Assuming that such projects are 'activated' as recovery measures during a period of depression, or at least recession, they come as manna to the construction goods industries during their period of famine. This is a bonanza for those industries. But owing to the action of the 'multiplier,' the restorative effect is transmitted to the whole industrial system. The flow of purchasing power, not only through the employees of the public works themselves, but also through those of the construction goods industries, has a stimulating effect on the whole business community.

But at this point we encounter the same difficulty which qualifies the influence of the interest rate. Is the flow of income through public works sufficient to sustain the economy continuously at the level of full employment? It is only if there is no limit to the extent of public works. That is, if it is assumed that the public works program will be expanded to whatever magnitude is necessary to achieve and maintain full employment, then such a program is adequate — by definition. But the indefinite extension of public works would very soon reach the point at which the projects would 'compete with private business.' No one imagines that full employment could be sustained by the public construction of swimming pools and courthouses. An unlimited program would necessarily extend to steel mills and locomotive works.

This actually happens in war. As everybody knows, during the recent war the government did in fact build steel mills, shipyards, airplane factories, and a myriad of similar establishments of the sort which private business ordinarily regards as falling within its jurisdiction. Private business tolerated such incursions, not without grumbling, as an incident of war and on the clear understanding that at the end of the war the government will dispose of all such plants and retire from the scene.

Would public works be accepted as a permanent arrangement if it were understood that no limits would be set to such a program, which therefore might involve governmental intrusion into private industry on a scale comparable to that of war? The answer, obviously, is No. The acceptability of public works is based on the quite definite and general presumption that such a program is to be limited to works already clearly identified as public: postoffices, courthouses, parks, and the like. The inclusion of steel mills and locomotive works would mean that under the guise of public works government jurisdiction was being extended over the whole of industry.

But if this were not in fact the case, there is no assurance of the flow of income being sufficient to sustain full production. The case of a limited program of public works is the same as that of the interest rate. What sustains the demand for industrial construction generally is the flow of mass-consumer purchasing power which constitutes demand for the end products of all industry. The construction of highways and school buildings might and should be planned so as to prevent the construction goods industries from multiplying the ill effects of dwindling consumer demand. But such limited relief could not possibly take the place of mass-consumer demand for the end products of all industry.

Consequently the alternative is clear. Either public construction must be unlimited and the not-very-gradual socialization of all industry must be accepted as the inevitable result, or some other way of increasing the flow of mass-consumer purchasing power must be adopted. If we follow the latter alternative, we can still make use of public works to offset the tendency of the construction goods industries to multiply our troubles. But our chief reliance must be placed on some means of rectifying the flow of income through the whole industrial economy.

17

Social Security

W HAT WE REQUIRE, and all we require, to make the industrial economy work is a flow of mass-consumer purchasing power sufficient to absorb the entire product of industry at whatever level of production we may be able to achieve. This would not bring utopia. It would not solve all problems. On the contrary, it would solve only one problem, the crisis into which we have been thrust by the institutions and dogmas of absolute capitalism. But this problem is the most important one we face today in this sense. If we solve this problem, we shall then have an opportunity to tackle others. If we do not, all our present problems will merge in the general collapse of the present structure of Western society.

As we know, increasing the flow of mass-consumer purchasing power means increasing the flow of income through small incomes, for this reason: the larger the income, the greater the proportion that is saved; the smaller the income, the greater the proportion that is spent. Hence the only effective way to increase the flow of mass-consumer purchasing power is to increase the smallest incomes — ideally, to create income where none at all exists at present.

This could be done by providing income for those who are not 'gainfully employed.' As it happens, the non-gainfully employed are rather numerous and fall into a variety of groups. In addition to the ablebodied unemployed, they include infants, young people who, though able to work at certain jobs, are still undergoing educational preparation for 'careers of larger usefulness,' housewives, the sick (including maternity cases), cripples, the infirm aged, and the like. These are our subjects.

These groups are very familiar, since they are the objects of concern in all programs of social security or social insurance 'and allied services,' to quote the title of the celebrated Beveridge Report. This familiarity has its advantages and also its disadvantages. It relieves the present discussion from any further effort of identification. But it also means that any discussion of the incomes of these groups will inevitably suffer from being conducted in the atmosphere of the poorhouse.

Security has often been denounced as a mean and unworthy goal, and taken by itself so it is. But there is no reason whatever for taking it as the end-all-be-all either of individual existence or of social progress. On the contrary, its importance both for individuals and for society derives from the fact that it is a means to fuller and richer life — whatever we may mean by such expressions. The higher spiritual values have little attraction for individuals whose children are starving; and if they seek assurance that their children will be fed, we have no right to assume that eating is the limit of their aspiration. Similarly, it must not be assumed that as a society we have adopted the ideal of the feeding-pen because we propose to increase consumption. Such an assumption overlooks what has been the dominating consideration throughout the entire discussion, namely, the requirements of the economy as a whole. It is because the continued existence of the industrial economy requires enlarged consumption that we propose such enlargement. From this point of view the poor are heaven-sent. Their interest and the common interest exactly coincide.

Nevertheless, charity may corrupt. Must it necessarily do so? The whole issue of social security, and perhaps the fate of industrial society itself, turns upon this distinction of 'may' and 'must.' The problem is one which no discussion of social security can avoid facing. For if it is true that providing people with incomes which they have not earned must necessarily debase their character, then we are forced to the conclusion that industrial society can be saved only by debasing a substantial part of the community. Such a price may be too much, and we may therefore be forced to conclude that even total revolution would be preferable.

Fortunately the evidence is unmistakably clear. Absolute capitalism itself provides the clearest sort of demonstration that unearned income does not necessarily corrupt. For if it does, then its victims must include all the recipients of income from capital. To be sure, these beneficiaries differ from the recipients of charity in two important respects. For the most part their incomes are considerably larger than any charity, and the receipt of income from investments is no bar to further earnings of any magnitude. That is, corporations do not decline to pay dividends to stockholders on the ground that the stockholders in question are already earning large incomes as engineers, physicians, attorneys, or active businessmen.

This point is of very great importance because it is the significant difference between income that corrupts and income that does not corrupt. It is the issue of the 'means test.' In spite of what Anatole France ironically called 'the characteristic generosity of the poor toward the rich,' nobody relishes making contributions to the upkeep of people who are better off than he is. Before we are moved to generosity we must be convinced that the object of our charity is truly needy — so much needier than ourselves as to make a refusal of assistance seem positively churlish. Public charity has inherited this inhibition from private charity, and social security has inherited it from public charity.

But this condition is doubly corrupting. In the first place, it is intensely humiliating for the recipient of the 'dole' to be obliged to make a more or less public exhibition of his indigence; and — even more important — it is definitely corrupting for the continued receipt of the 'dole' to be contingent upon the continuance of the indigence. This means that any opportunity to earn must necessarily be weighed against the loss of public assistance which it may entail.

History affords some truly appalling instances of the effects of such a policy. One of the worst and most bitterly controversial was the system, known as the 'Speenhamland system,' set up in England in 1795 and in force for several decades thereafter. One writer makes this system primarily responsible for the rise of British socialism; but others point out that although Speenhamland did encourage indigence by withdrawing assistance from people who were making the first feeble efforts to help themselves, it also saved many from starvation by setting a (very low) minimum of subsistence below which no one was allowed to fall. True, it encouraged illegitimacy by a dole that was contingent upon bearing a child. Stories were told of women who had had four illegitimate children and said they would be 'sitting pretty' if they could only have one more. Nevertheless, the system was sufficiently humane to try to save even the illegitimate from starvation.

Such is the dilemma which social security has inherited from private charity. What is wrong here is a confusion of motives. No parent would think of sending his child supperless to bed on the ground that he had gone out during the afternoon and earned fifty cents mowing other people's lawns and therefore had lost his claim on an equivalent amount of family largess. Why? Surely the reason is that parents identify themselves with the personalities and fortunes of their children. The better off the children are, the better pleased the parents are — and with reason.

This is precisely the case with industrial society and its smallest consumers. The more incomes are increased at the bottom of the scale, the larger is mass consumption; and the larger mass consumption is, the better off everybody is.

True, the case of the giver of private charity is quite different. He gives without thought or hope of any but spiritual advantage. What he gives is a total loss to him, financially at least. No common financial interest identifies his interests with those of the recipient of his bounty. Consequently he has a valid reason for adjusting his benefaction to the proved need of its recipient and reducing it or discontinuing it altogether as that need diminishes; and all modern systems of public relief and social security have inherited that motivation from the private giver.

Our dilemma is historical. Our present need is to effect a substantially greater flow of mass-consumer purchasing power. To do so will mean economic salvation for all of us. Not to do so will mean common disaster. We do have the same common interest in the enlargement of the consumption of low-income groups which parents have in the improvement of their children. But the administrative apparatus for doing this still bears the taint of private charity.

What we have to do, obviously, is to modernize our motives and our apparatus. There is no reason whatever why unearned income should corrupt if we do not want it to corrupt. If we do not — and we had better not! — all we have to do is to treat the community as we treat our children. No one will endure hard labor to make twenty dollars a week when he can receive twenty-five if he has no other source of income and will lose it if he has any sort of job. But no one in his senses will refuse a job that means doubling his income.

It is sometimes argued that recipients of charity are literally senseless. Alas, some of them are. Some are indigent because they have been born senseless. Others have been driven senseless by poverty. But such cases have no bearing whatever on the pros and cons of social security. It would be ridiculous to argue that social security will debase its subjects because some were born debased and others have been incurably debased by antecedent conditions. One might just as well argue that medical care is no good since some diseases are hereditary and some cases of illness are already so far advanced that medicine can do nothing for them.

No policy is sound which does not assume that other people are very much like oneself. Well-to-do people do not desist from earning more because they already have something, and neither will ill-to-do people. Obviously the thing to do to make a social security program wholly effective is to extend its benefits to the entire population irrespective of their earnings and even of their other independent income.

The Beveridge Report proposes to do precisely this for the people of Great Britain, abolishing the infamous 'means test' and blanketing the entire population into the system. This is made easy by the fact that the system takes the form of insurance — a perfectly respectable and familiar device. But the effect would be the same if governmental funds were the source of the entire flow of income which the system would set up instead of 'matching' the contributions (or premiums) paid by each individual member.

Such a system would be the most direct, effective, and economical way to supplement the flow of income in small-income channels. Virtually every dollar would go just where the economy needs it. For even if old-age benefits were paid to millionaires, we must remember, first, that millionaires are few in number and, secondly, that progressive taxation (the subject of the next chapter) would recapture every dollar and redirect it toward the vast number of small incomes.

Furthermore, such a system is perfectly flexible. Nothing is involved but money income, and of all forms of wealth money is the most liquid. The flow of income which the system would set up could be increased or decreased as circumstances dictate. Indeed, unemployment payments, which should, of course, be one of the most important instrumentalities of the whole system, would automatically increase and decrease as employment decreased and increased, without a single penny ever being diverted to millionaires. (Some evidence of the fact of unemployment would, of course, be required under such a system; but it could and should have reference to regular employment, and it need not and should not involve any means-test snooping into the amount of its subjects' savings or any other sources of income such as odd jobs or substitute employment.)

All this is generally admitted. That is, nobody denies that a program such as we have come to identify by the phrase 'social security' would set up a flow of increased income in small-income channels, or that such a flow of income would be subject to flexible control. To be sure, Sir William Beveridge does express some hesitation in his recent sequel to the Report, *Full Employment in a Free Society*; and since he is the greatest living exponent of what the Report called 'social insurance and allied services,' his misgivings are worth quoting in full.

> Some expansion of private outlay [he says on page 184], brought about by a redistribution of income increasing the propensity to consume, should be a part of a full-employment policy. Several of the measures included in the program of spending set out above, in particular those for Social Security, would have this consequence. The proposal to be examined here goes further. It is that the placing of adequate purchasing power in the hands of the citizens, so that they will spend more, should be the main instrument of a full-employment policy. It is argued that in this way full employment might be achieved with a minimum of State interference and planning. To a proposal of this character there are several serious objections.

In the pages immediately following, Beveridge cites two objections. One of these is that consumption so induced 'might not be wisely directed' or 'might not be directed to those forms of consumption which were socially most desirable,' and he mentions a variety of possible unwise and undesirable expenditures. The other 'and most important' objection is that 'there are many essential services which individuals either cannot get for themselves or can get only at excessive cost,' such as 'nursery schools, playgrounds, hospitals, libraries, . . . good housing in healthy surroundings.'

These, he insists, are 'vital needs which can be met only by collective action.'

These misgivings with regard to the wisdom and social vision of much of our consumption, and also with regard to the commercial accessibility of important services to the private consumer, are of course wholly justified. No one would deny that even the highest measure of continuous and continuously rising prosperity would leave many persistent problems to be dealt with — educational and moral problems of every sort. Nor would anyone deny that social services such as those indicated would not be automatically provided by prosperity or that continued vigilant effort would be required to secure them.

But if these problems would not be solved by the achievement of full employment, neither would full employment be achieved by attention to these problems. Our great respect for Sir William Beveridge must not be allowed to conceal the plain fact that his objections are quite irrelevant. They amount to saying that social security is not the sum total of human effort. But who says it is? Social security is not the sum total of human effort because full employment is not the sum total of human aspiration. Social security is the way to get full employment. Nothing Sir William says casts the slightest doubt on that proposition. He only says that we must eventually set our sights higher than full employment, which of course is true, but quite another story.

Other objections are indeed made, with the greatest vigor and even bitterness. They are capitalistic objections. People who deny the possibility of general unemployment object to social security or any other program for preventing what they deny exists. So do people who attribute unemployment to 'government interference.' People who maintain that the

Administration which began in 1933 was responsible for the depression which began in 1929 also object to social security.

If objections such as these prevail, they will make any adequate program of social security 'politically' impossible. That does not mean that it is economically impossible. It is perfectly feasible, economically. There is no serious economic obstacle to the immediate realization of full employment and continuously rising prosperity. The objections of economic royalists would only mean that absolute capitalism would come to an end in the United States as absolute monarchy came to an end in France and Russia, and not as it came to an end in England. Our economic royalists have it in their power to prevent the realization of limited capitalism. They do not have it in their power to preserve absolute capitalism. Nothing can do that.

18

Progressive Taxation

'WHERE IS THE MONEY COMING FROM?' 'Who is going to bear the cost?' 'Is there enough money even in the whole economy to carry the dead weight of such a program?'

Questions such as these are often heard even today. As questions they are, of course, legitimate. But in so far as such questions suggest misgivings, they are based on a complete misconception, not only of the corrective measures under discussion, but also of the underlying condition we are seeking to correct. Indeed, this misconception is so completely at variance with the plain facts as to justify the suspicion that people who seek to arouse such misgivings intend to confuse public discussion and obstruct corrective action.

In the first place, measures calculated to redress the flow of income would not be a dead weight. On the contrary, it is the present income differential — the tendency of income to flow faster into large-income channels than into small-income channels — that is a burden. That burden is so heavy that it threatens to sink the whole economy. The whole object of corrective measures is to lighten the dead weight of that burden.

105

Such lightening of the income burden involves a double adjustment. Income must be made to flow faster into small-income channels. It has been the object of the preceding chapters to show that this can be done most directly and effectively by a program of social security, though other measures would contribute to the same effect and should, of course, be used for whatever they are worth to supplement social security. But income must also be made to flow more slowly into large-income channels. The two channels are, of course, complementary. It is because under the institutions and ideas of capitalism too much income flows into large incomes that too little flows into small ones — too little to absorb the product of industry. The need to reduce large incomes is just as pressing as the need to increase small ones. The two adjustments complement each other.

This is the answer to another of the obstructive questions, 'Where is the money coming from?' It is coming from large incomes, of course. Unless that is the case, small incomes will not have been increased relatively to large ones. To tax small incomes to support a program of social security would be a sheer waste of effort. The left hand would take away what the right hand giveth, and the only net result would be saddling the community with the administrative cost of making totally useless motions.

Since the whole object of the effort to redress the flow of income is to increase the volume of consumption, the worst tax that could be devised is a general sales tax. Not only is such a tax regressive, resting more heavily on small incomes than on large ones; it places an obstacle directly in the way of consumer spending, the very thing we need to increase.

The perfect instrument for reducing the flow of income to large incomes is the direct progressive taxation of personal incomes. This is true virtually by definition, since such taxation is assessed directly on the recipients of income and is graduated according to the amount of income. It is well illustrated by the *rates* of the present federal personal income tax. Incomes smaller than a specified minimum are not taxed at all. Those just above this minimum are taxed only a small per cent of the 'net taxable income' which remains after various deductions and allowances have been made, and the per cent taken by the tax increases until it reaches a maximum at which something like nine-tenths may (theoretically) be taken. Thus, the recipient of a million-dollar-a-year income (and this would be realized by a five per cent return on a fortune of twenty million dollars) is left to scrape along on something like one hundred thousand dollars a year.

No one doubts the possible effectiveness of direct progressive taxation. The only limit to the amount of funds it could draw off from the sum of personal incomes of the community is the sum total of all incomes. Tax experts often couple the income tax with the inheritance, or estate, tax. To tax incomes but not inheritances would, of course, be utterly inconsistent. But special provision for taxing inheritances is necessary only if such acquisitions have been specifically exempted from income taxation. If inheritances were treated like all other income and taxed as such, no special tax would be required. And why not? If a writer 'hits the jackpot' with a successful play, he may make half a million dollars in one year, all of which is taxable as personal income. If his neighbor inherits half a million, that is subject to estate taxation only. Why the difference? To be sure, an answer can be given in terms of the sacredness of capital funds, but in terms of their effect on the economy all such windfalls are identical.

Our concern is solely with the amount of income, not at all with its source. That is what income taxation takes account of, and that is all it takes account of, and it takes complete account of it.

Even so, the question may still be raised whether income taxation would provide funds enough to raise consumption to the necessary level. In dealing with this question, three things must be borne in mind.

First, nobody expects the stream of income that is diverted from large incomes to small ones by progressive taxation and social security to be the only source of mass-consumer purchasing power. By far the greater part of the flow of consumer purchasing power will be through ordinary channels of wages, salaries, and the like. Nobody even expects the diversionary stream to be the whole, or even the greater part, of the increase of mass-consumer purchasing power. The greater part of the increase will also flow through ordinary channels, into which it will be released by the 'multiplier' effect of the diversionary flow. All that is expected of the diversionary flow is that it shall activate the multiplier.

The incomes of the very rich, though large, are far from numerous. If the question were only by how much the incomes of the poor would be increased if all the incomes of all the rich and even the moderately well-to-do were distributed among the poor, the answer would be quite unsatisfactory. But that is not the question. The question is how to maintain full and continually rising production. If it is true that our failure to do this in the past has resulted from the differential flow of income, then the object of the proposed diversionary flow is to overcome that differential. Only that. Nothing more.

Secondly, we must never forget Say's law. According to this venerable maxim, production must always create its own sufficient market. Whatever the sums laid out in production, they are paid to the 'factors of production,' by whom in turn they are either spent or invested; and so they flow back into the market, purchasing consumers' goods and capital goods in quantities precisely commensurate with the total volume of production.

For nearly a century and a half this 'law' has been the mainstay of the belief that private business can maintain full employment. We now know that Say's law does not hold. But it fails to hold, not because funds are deficient in the aggregate, but because faulty distribution of income permits (and even obliges) some funds to be accumulated for which no real investment in actual capital goods can be made. This impediment is due to the deficiency of consumer purchasing power, a deficiency which is caused by the excess flow of funds into large incomes and is precisely commensurate to it.

Thus, the amount of funds which it is necessary to divert from large incomes is exactly equal to the amount of oversaving; that is, spurious investment and outright hoarding. If we could infallibly detect hoarding and spurious investment, the recapture of those very funds would be sufficient to maintain full production and employment. But hoarding is almost impossible to detect, spurious investment quite impossible. Nobody ever knows whether his investments are 'good' except as subsequent events reveal — or even determine — their character. Even if detection were possible, it would perhaps be unreasonably harsh to penalize the follies of investors by total confiscation. (That is what bankruptcy does; but a responsible social policy must be juster than outrageous fortune.) Consequently, we have no alternative but to treat all recipients of large incomes as potential hoarders or 'suckers' in direct ratio to the size of their incomes, diverting from the sum total of their incomes by progressive rates an amount equivalent to the oversaving with which their incomes threaten us.

At this point we might well pause to consider an objection. The objection which is urged most vigorously against effectively progressive income taxation is that such a levy would cut down the flow of investment funds at their large-income source and so would kill the financial goose that lays the industrial golden eggs. This objection is a perfect example of capitalistic dogma. For it is valid only on the assumption that all accumulated funds necessarily become real investments, and as such inevitably expand industry and provide enlarged employment. It is a sound objection only on the assumption that there is no such thing as depression, not to mention war and revolution. But on the assumption that such conditions do exist and are to be explained by the differential flow of income, the objection has no force whatever. The diversion of funds in the amount of hoarding and spurious investment cannot possibly reduce the volume of real investment. One might as well argue that the removal of counterfeit money from circulation will deprive business of the necessary volume of currency.

Since hoarding and spurious investment escape immediate detection, they provide no means of measuring the total amount of oversaving and so of ascertaining the point to which the diversion of income should be carried. But there are other ways by which this point can be quite definitely recognized. One is by the price-level. When the general price-level begins to rise sharply, as it does under war conditions owing to the failure of production of consumers' goods to keep pace with consumer purchasing power, obviously a cutback is called for. And the same is true of the interest rate. The moment the point is reached at which a scarcity of funds available for real investment begins to develop, competing businesses will bid against each other for existing savings by raising their offers of interest, and this is another indication of the saturation point.

But full employment is the best indication. When the diversion of funds from large-income channels to small-income channels has, with the assistance of the multiplier, raised the total flow of mass-consumer purchasing power to such a volume that all the goods are being bought which can then be made by employment of the full manpower of the community, obviously no further increase will serve a useful purpose. At such a point the flow of funds through social security channels will have undergone considerable reduction, as we have seen; and so a treasury surplus will be growing fast. This in itself is a sufficient cue for tax reduction.

Thus, a third consideration must also be kept in mind. Throughout the foregoing discussion the diversion of funds has been treated as though it would involve an absolute reduction of large incomes. But it is very doubtful if this is the case. For the diversion we have been discussing would greatly increase the entire social income produced by the economy as a whole. That is the object of the whole maneuver. The fluctuations of which the social income is capable are very great. In 1929 the national income of the United States was eighty-three billion dollars. In 1932 it was forty billions. In 1939 it had reached seventy-one billions. From this point it rose to one hundred and forty-eight billions in 1943. There is every likelihood that a rate of increase of several billions a year could be maintained indefinitely. If this were to be achieved, it would mean in all probability that no absolute reduction of the flow of income in large-income channels would ever actually take place. What would happen would be a reduction of the rate of increase from the excessive rate which absolute capitalism enforces to a more moderate rate of increase commensurate with the growth of the social income and the expansion of real investment opportunities based on a commensurately increasing flow of mass-consumer purchasing power.

The importance of this point is impossible to exaggerate. The facts are plain, and they have been pointed out again and again by witnesses of undeniable qualifications and unimpeachable integrity. They have, nevertheless, been persistently ignored simply and solely because they are disastrously embarrassing to absolute capitalism. Thus, it has been pointed out repeatedly that the entire cost of all the recovery agencies of the nineteen-thirties was never more than a moderate fraction of the increase of the national income by which they were accompanied. The fact that some of those agencies are generally admitted to have been far from ideally effective — some of them even worked against each other — only serves to emphasize the tremendous significance of a rising national income. Obviously, full employment is a very good bargain indeed for all the participants — even the recipients of incomes whose rate of increase must be curtailed. Even they will enjoy increasing incomes; and the still greater possible (though temporary) increase which they do not get, they will not subsequently lose.

So potent is a rising social income that it has often been

cited as a sufficient offset to a perpetually rising debt and even to a perpetually expanding paper currency. Both of these claims are true, but neither is a decisive reason for adopting such a policy in preference to direct taxation.

The objection to financing a long-range economic program by borrowing is not the size of the debt that would result. The public hullabaloo over the size of the national debt is scare-fool demagoguery. The people who raise the outcry know better, as witness their complacency in the face of a war debt more than four times larger than the amount they set during the nineteen-thirties as the absolute maximum, to go one dollar beyond which would surely mean utter bankruptcy. Obviously, what they really feared was not the size of the debt, but the purpose for which it was then being assumed.

Economists are pretty well agreed that the size of the national debt is immaterial, for this reason: every bond is an asset as well as a liability. In this respect public debt is exactly like private debt. If the community is the debtor, the community is also the creditor in the same amount (assuming, to avoid international complications, that the debt is domestically held, as is true of our national debt).

It is true, of course, that responsibility for paying and claims to be paid may be distributed differently. If we assume that the bonds are owned by the rich and the well-to-do in proportion to their fortunes, and if we also assume that every citizen bears an equal responsibility for retiring these bonds, then obviously ninety-nine per cent of the population is in bondage — not to 'the state,' but to the other one per cent. But such would be the case, not by virtue of the existence of a debt, but only by virtue of our assumptions with regard to the distribution of assets and liabilities. In actual fact it still remains to be determined in what fashion our financial responsibilities will be distributed. That will be determined by future taxation. If future revenue acts place chief reliance on direct progressive taxation of personal incomes, that will mean the distribution of the burden of taxation on a pattern exactly coinciding with what we have assumed to be the distribution of claims to repayment, and will therefore represent no burden at all.

But if this can be done to retire a debt, why could it not be done in the first place to finance an economic program and even a war? The answer is, It could. Every program, even including war, is in fact financed out of current income. What makes the bond sales possible, if not current income? It is quite untrue that the cost of war is saddled on future generations. What is saddled on future generations is the cost of retiring the bonds — an utterly different proposition. We borrow, not because taxation on such a scale is economically impossible, but only because we are politically unready to decide where to put the burden of taxation. Borrowing postpones that decision. But since taxation is the inevitable subject of the ultimate decision, that is the issue to which our thinking should be addressed — now no less than later. For if our minds were made up with regard to that issue of principle, postponement by borrowing would be unnecessary.

In considerable part, however, government bonds are not sold to individual buyers and are not purchased out of current income. They are sold to banks which create the money with which to pay for them, using the bonds as collateral for the issuance of created credit. To this (very large) extent the war has been financed by currency (checking account) expansion. This operation is perfectly safe, since it is accompanied by, and indeed is the cause of, a very great increase of the national income incident to the war effort. Scarcity of consumers' goods, due to wartime curtailment of civilian production, is what sends prices up.

A long-range program of income diversion such as we have been discussing would also mean the continuous increase of the national income, and with no curtailment of production to send prices up. Consequently, the proposal has been made that such a program might well be financed by this maneuver. This would indeed be possible. That is, a rising national income would make it possible for government to create the funds with which to finance the flow of mass-consumer purchasing power through social security.

But this maneuver would not divert any funds from large-income channels. Consequently, its effectiveness would be only half that of a combined program of social security financed by direct progressive taxation. To be sure, it could be supplemented by such taxation, just as borrowing could be followed by taxation. But if this is to be done, it might just as well be done from the outset, in which case the fund-creating maneuver would be unnecessary and pointless. For that maneuver, like the borrowing to which it is closely related, is primarily a stop-gap postponement of the real decision.

The decision is, of course, momentous. No nation has ever employed direct progressive taxation on such a scale. We have recognized the principle. The rates of our present federal personal income tax embody that principle. Nevertheless, existing income taxes fail to provide funds in any such volume as would be required to redress the balance of the economy. This fact is sometimes cited as evidence that sufficient funds do not exist. But what it proves is the extreme faultiness of present income taxes.

The trouble is that wide avenues of escape have been provided. These avenues are well known, not only to all students of taxation, but to all those who utilize them to escape taxation. All that is necessary for a fortune to escape income taxation altogether is that it should consist of tax-exempt bonds. In the early nineteen-thirties some of the greatest fortunes in the country escaped taxation altogether by deducting capital losses from current income. Earnings may escape personal income taxation by remaining in a business as undivided surplus — hence the frantic, and successful, opposition to a recent (short-lived) tax on undivided surplus. Even the salaries of top executives may escape the high rates of the personal income tax by assuming the form of grants of stock or options to buy stock at less than market prices.

But there is no need for an inventory of the defects of past and present revenue acts. The point is that defects exist and are known to be defects. That is why they were enacted. Just as in the case of the historic doles and poor laws, we have in a fashion distributed relief, but have taken care to do so in such a fashion as to make the whole business as opprobrious as possible, so in the case of direct progressive taxation we have gone through the motions of accepting the principle and enacting the tax (even passing a constitutional amendment to make it a part of the American Way of Life), but have taken care to do so in such a way as to defeat the operation of the principle on which we have purported to be acting.

Our failure has been a failure of nerve due to fear of the unknown. For an effective program of income diversion would mean the voluntary abandonment of absolute capitalism. It would also mean, not total revolution, but the voluntary adoption of limited capitalism.

Nevertheless, this is the direction in which we have been moving for many years, carried forward in large part by our historic talent — as old as the industrial revolution — for gradual transition. It only remains for us to take the decisive step.

PART III

LIMITED CAPITALISM

19

An Economy That Works

Wʜᴀᴛ would limited capitalism look like? If we should come to realize at last that accumulated funds are not the divine source from which all blessings flow, and if we should therefore take the necessary steps to rectify the flow of income, what would the consequences be? What sort of scene would greet the eyes of an observer who stood looking up and down the Main Street of a typical American community?

These questions can be answered very simply and with considerable certainty. Such an observer would detect no differences from the scenes with which he had been familiar all his life. To all outward appearances business would be going on very much as usual. All up and down the street private businessmen would be offering goods for sale in the familiar ways, and shoppers would be hunting for bargains after the long-accustomed manner of their kind.

All this might bring a shock of disappointment to any Rip Van Winkle who had gone to sleep in the belief that any change must lead to total change, with universal rationing and long queues waiting for their turn at the meager and unappetizing shelves of government commissaries. Some such notion as this has been sedulously promoted by people who are opposed to any change. The experiences of travelers in the Soviet Union have seemed to give it plausibility, and on a much larger scale so have our own experiences in wartime.

But such a reading of those experiences is exactly upside down. As we all know, it was scarcity due to the war that made rationing necessary and obliged people to stand in line for things — 'one to a customer.' To be sure, we could have put an end to all that sort of thing at any time by leaving everything to 'the laws of supply and demand.' Mink coats are scarce at all times. But we never see poor people standing in line for them, one to a customer. Their prices ration them to people who can pay the price, including the price of not being kept waiting. Meat and sugar, tires and gasoline, could have been distributed mink-coat-wise, but not to war workers. We rationed scarce goods in wartime to insure that the entire war-working community would be fed and clothed and transported to and from work. The Soviet Union did the same thing for the same reason even in peacetime. In both cases the basic condition is that of scarcity — general scarcity of staple consumers' goods.

But the condition from which we suffer perennially under absolute capitalism is the precise reverse, namely, the continual threat of 'overproduction' — that is to say, underconsumption. Rationing goods and making customers queue up at special commissaries would be a strange way of dealing with a surfeit. What we need, year in and year out, is not more goods than we can make, but more customers than we can find. True, Sir William Beveridge's definition of full employment as a sellers' market for labor also means a sellers' market for goods. If the flow of income were adjusted so as to provide enough consumer purchasing power to absorb the full product of industry, there would be no more depression bargains, because there would be no more sacrifice sales. But this would not mean that there would be any need for rationing or any other major alteration of the familiar shopping scene.

Limited capitalism would nevertheless be profoundly different from the absolute capitalism of the past few centuries. But its differences would not be visible, so to speak, from the corner of Broadway and Main Street. This is true primarily because they would not be apparent at any particular moment of time, since they are matters of time.

Under limited capitalism there would be no more depressions. The reason for this is already clear. Supplemented by the 'independent incomes' which social security would inject into the economy at those points at which hitherto income has been almost totally deficient and where as a consequence virtually every dollar would be spent, the flow of mass-consumer purchasing power would absorb the entire product of industry. This would mean full employment; and since there is nothing temporary or contingent about any part of this flow of income, it would mean continuous full employment. Any lay-offs that might result from any sort of industrial change-over, such as the retooling which automobile manufacturers must do when a new model is introduced, would back up a reservoir of unsatisfied consumer demand, just as war conditions are now doing. This reservoir of unspent purchasing power, supplemented by the flow of social security payments to the unemployed, would force prices up, just as unsatisfied demand does under war conditions; and this would force a resumption of production, employment, and a renewed flow of purchasing power through wage channels.

Meantime the flow of income through large-income channels would be correspondingly reduced. Consequently, there would be no excess of funds seeking investment opportunities beyond those which full production would provide. Hence there would be no unhealthy boom on the stock exchange, no pronounced upward movement of security prices, and no squandering of funds in worthless investments. More fundamentally, there would be no possibility of a renewal of the differential flow of income whereby large incomes have increased faster than small incomes with a consequent relative decline of consumer purchasing power. Income would flow steadily in both directions.

None of these differences would be very startling or dramatic at any given moment. They would be present at all times; they would be observed with interest by statisticians, and would no doubt be the subject of violent controversy among economic theorists for many years. No doubt some would continue to argue that no significant change had occurred, and even when the passage of time had made it unmistakably clear that a 'normal cyclical fluctuation' (that is, a depression) had been skipped, some would still find old-fashioned explanations for this phenomenon. In the meantime life would still seem to casual observers very much what it has been (for all those who have been members of the American economy) during past periods of prosperity. A profound change would have taken place. The present crisis of capitalism would have been passed. But it might take years — decades, even, or perhaps generations — for the community to become fully aware of this.

All this is also true of war, and in even greater degree.

We dare not say that under limited capitalism there would be no more war. So long as old ambitions fester and old hatreds smoulder, war is still a possibility. Furthermore, limited capitalism might be achieved in some countries, but absolute capitalism might continue to prevail in others, which would therefore still be potential disturbers of the peace. But for the countries which adopted it, limited capitalism would bring immediate relief from the necessity which has made recurrent war inevitable throughout modern times.

This is, of course, the necessity to find foreign outlets for 'surplus' goods, 'surplus' funds, and even 'surplus' population. Under limited capitalism there would be no such surpluses. All would be employed. Full production would provide investment opportunities sufficient to absorb the whole of the (somewhat diminished) volume of funds accumulated for investment. And the flow of mass-consumer purchasing power would be sufficient to absorb the entire produce of industry at full production in the domestic market.

This would not mean that all domestically produced goods must be domestically consumed with nothing left over for export and therefore no possibility of obtaining foreign products by trading for them with our own. What is significant is the total volume of production balanced by the total volume of consumption. Any 'even-Stephen' trade of our goods for other countries' goods would be perfectly possible and desirable, since it would give us — and them — the advantage of regional specialization without affecting the balance of production and consumption in either country. In the words of J. M. Keynes,

> There would still be room for the international division of labor and for international lending in appropriate condi-

tions. But there would no longer be a pressing motive why one country need force its wares on another or repulse the offerings of its neighbor, not because this was necessary to enable it to pay for what it wished to purchase, but with the express object of upsetting the equilibrium of payments so as to develop a balance of trade in its own favor. International trade would cease to be what it is, namely, a desperate expedient to maintain employment at home by forcing sales on foreign markets and restricting purchases, which, if successful, will merely shift the problem of unemployment to the neighbor which is worsted in the struggle; but a willing and unimpeded exchange of goods and services in conditions of mutual advantage.

For the United States to achieve this condition would not bring complete relief to the entire world. But as Alvin Hansen says, 'This country could make no greater contribution toward the solution of the international political as well as economic problems than that of achieving a high degree of internal stability at a level of fairly full employment of labor and other resources.' For we must never forget the magnitude of the American economy. This is what Hansen has in mind as he continues, 'It is, I think, a fact that the extraordinary instability of the American economy presents one of the most serious problems confronting Europe and, indeed, the whole world.' The same opinion is expressed even more forcefully, and for the same reason, by Sir William Beveridge. 'The adoption of a policy of full employment by the United States,' he says, 'would be the most important economic advance that could happen in the whole world and to the benefit of the whole world.'

Nevertheless, the source of this benefit, great as it is, would not be immediately apparent. For like depression, war is an occasional phenomenon. Indeed, the war cycle is even longer than the depression cycle. People who confidently expect another global war nevertheless allow two or three decades for it to develop, and their expectations might survive for a much longer time. After all, a century elapsed between the global wars of the Napoleonic era and those of our time.

Meantime, as in the case of depression, another explanation could be given for the lengthening peace, in this case a political explanation. If, as now seems possible, the United Nations should become a reality, the preservation of the peace might be attributed to that body, and with considerable justice. After all, the United Nations may actually be the agency through which the economic policies of limited capitalism are realized.

This is already true of the Bretton Woods agreements. In the preceding discussion no account has been taken of the possibility of using exports to maintain full employment, since there is no such possibility. Dumping exports on foreign markets does sustain production for a time. But it does this by what Lord Keynes called 'exporting unemployment.' That practice — the necessity, as it has seemed, of resorting to foreign markets to relieve domestic 'overproduction' — has been the principal cause of all the major wars of modern times, as we have already noted. To prevent such a one-way flow of exports in excess of imports by substituting administrative controls for the unregulated (or unilaterally manipulated) gold standard is the primary object of the agencies set up by the Bretton Woods agreements.

This change is typical of limited capitalism in being far more significant than appears on the surface. The contrary practice, that of dumping excess exports on foreign markets, has prevailed throughout the entire history of capitalism and

has been an inevitable corollary of capitalist ideas and institutions. Professor Heckscher has pointed out in his monu-
mental study of *Mercantilism* that 'exporting unemployment'
was not only systematically practiced, but was so understood, as far back as the end of the sixteenth century. In
theory *laissez faire* was a complete break with mercantilism.
In theory free exchange of goods and currencies under the
gold standard meant an automatic balance of exports and
imports. But in practice, as we know, the more highly industrialized countries enjoyed an advantage which the unregulated gold standard allowed them to exploit to the limit,
with results which are now only too familiar.

What is now proposed is thus a reversal of the practice
that has prevailed continuously hitherto. Whereas hitherto
foreign trade has responded to the (supposed) necessities of
the domestic economy, it is now proposed that the domestic
economy shall respond to the real and obvious necessity of
a balance of exports and imports in foreign trade. This in
itself means limited capitalism. Nobody says so. Certainly
nobody calls it that. To outward appearances the only
change is the prospective creation of an international bank
and a stabilization fund. Limited capitalism is only the climate in which such institutions grow.

The same is true of the Charter of the United Nations.
This achievement is highly conditional. As everybody sees,
the success of the Charter depends altogether upon the
'good will' of the great powers. A cynic might say of it, 'If
two small powers fight, the organization steps in, and that is
the end of the fight; if a small power and a big power fight,
that is the end of the small power; unless, of course, another
big power steps in, and that is the end of the organization.'
That is, the Charter will succeed if it is the instrument by
which limited capitalism is realized.

If absolute capitalism persists unabated, conflict between the great powers will be inevitable sooner or later. It will not be inevitable, and the Charter will 'work,' only if the other great powers achieve domestic equilibrium as the Soviet Union has already done through the drastic methods of communist revolution. They may eventually be driven to such a course. On the other hand, they may achieve equilibrium while avoiding the horrors of total revolution through limited capitalism. If this happens, doubtless the Charter will get the credit for the world security which will then ensue.

For limited capitalism is a negative condition. Like limited monarchy, it is only the old and familiar setup purged of its worst features; and since its worst features — wars and depressions — are occasional by nature, even their absence might not be noticed for some time. Meantime things would go on very much as before. Certainly limited capitalism would not be utopia. Folly and cruelty, injustice and corruption, would still persist. A considerable part of the community would still lead relatively meager lives — relatively, that is, to the level of the most fortunate members of the community.

Nevertheless, the level of the community, and especially the bottom level, would be far higher than it has ever been. For all the members of the community would be members of the industrial economy. What this means was very clearly put by the editors of *Fortune Magazine* in February, 1940, when they devoted their decennial issue to a survey of the American economy. It was a most impressive survey. Even at that time the achievements of American industry were prodigious. Compared with existence in other countries, not to mention other ages, it was evident that the American people, even the common people, 'led the life of Riley.' Even so, there were at that time 9,377,000 unemployed who with their families made up a population block of thirty million souls. This phenomenon was too large to be ignored, and credit must be given to the editors for devoting a section of their survey to it under the heading, 'The Dispossessed.' What they said about these people was especially significant. These people, they said, are not really members of the American economy. 'The American system, as is made clear throughout this issue, works better than any other in the world — for the 77 per cent who belong to it. This story is about the other 23 per cent. . . . For nearly one-fourth of the population there is no economic system — and from the rest there is no answer.' Total membership is part of the answer limited capitalism would give.

Raising the bottom level is another part. In 1934, the Brookings Institution estimated that production in 1929, the peak year prior to the recent war, fell some 19 per cent short of existing capacity, or about fifteen billion dollars; and that additional production of this amount, if it had been distributed among the 70 per cent of the families of the nation with incomes ranging from zero to twenty-five hundred dollars, would have been sufficient to bring all of them up to a twenty-five-hundred-dollar minimum.

Obviously, this would be a magnificent achievement. It would mean wiping abject poverty out of existence. But even so, the most important part of the answer still remains. What is most important is the total volume of production. The figures given by the Brookings Institution contemplated an increase of fifteen billion dollars over actual production in 1929. But by the end of the war American industry had reached a rate of production something like double that of

1929. If such a volume of production could be turned into peacetime channels, and if it likewise were used to build up consumption at the bottom, how high could the bottom level of the American community be raised? No one has yet determined. The 1934 estimate of the Brookings Institution was that 'an increase of one thousand dollars in the consumptive expenditures of all families under the ten thousand dollar level would amount to about twenty-seven billion dollars.' At that rate peacetime production at the recent wartime peak would suffice to bring the bottom level of the whole community up to the vicinity of forty-five hundred dollars.

These are dream figures. But it is the American dream. It means no more than the full realization of the American Way of Life. If limited capitalism becomes an actuality, the well-fed, well-dressed, and generally well-cared-for citizens to be seen going about their familiar concerns on any Main Street will differ very little from their counterparts today. Only their numbers will be different.

20

Financing Industrial Growth

In MORE THAN ONE of the preceding chapters the proposition has been advanced that industrial growth does not depend on the accumulation of sums of money. Industrial growth is a consequence of the advancement of industrial technology. Without invention and discovery no amount of money could bring about industrial growth, and no real technical advance has ever been lost for lack of money.

Nevertheless, ours is a money economy as well as an industrial economy. Even under limited capitalism private investors would still hold the pursestrings. Consequently, we are confronted with a question we have not faced hitherto. How is industrial growth financed, and how would it be financed under limited capitalism? In spite of being a compound sentence, this is only one question. For under limited capitalism industrial growth would continue to be financed just as it has been in the past. Generally speaking, this is by the private accumulation of funds for the purpose of investment.

If we take this view of the problem, the question is whether such private accumulation would be sufficient under limited capitalism to keep pace with the industrial growth which invention and discovery make possible. This question can be approached from two directions, the demands of the economy and the effects of limited capitalism.

The effects which limited capitalism would have on private saving have already been considered at some length. Diversion of income from large incomes to small incomes would reduce the total amount of capital (fund) accumulation. It would not and could not reduce the amount available for real investment in actual (physical) industrial expansion. This difference is the difference between saving and oversaving. One of the two complementary objects of income diversion is to prevent functionless oversaving by reducing the flow of income to large incomes to the point at which the amount of funds accumulated is exactly equal to the investment requirements of the economy. The significance of full employment is its clear indication of that point. If full employment is desirable at all, it is desirable as a balance between saving and investment. If it does in fact perform this function, it cannot possibly reduce saving below the industrial needs of the community.

This implies that the demands of the economy are for more investment opportunities, not more savings. That has been the case throughout modern times. We often speak of an individual businessman, and of an undeveloped region, as needing capital, but in all such cases the need is much more general than the word 'capital' implies. An undeveloped region needs development. If it is an unpopulated frontier, what it needs quite as much as anything else is population. If it is a populous but industrially backward region, what it needs is a change in the attitudes and aptitudes of the people quite as much as funds. To say of an individual businessman that he needs capital (funds) is usually a polite way of saying that he needs 'gumption.' He will not be able to build up a business, and keep it, unless he 'has what it takes' to be a successful administrator; and if he were a successful administrator, he could get funds.

The perennial dearth of the economy as a whole has been a dearth, not of funds, but of investment opportunities. That is why in good times there has always been a vast outpouring of funds into undeveloped regions and undeveloped businesses, while in bad times there has been a correspondingly vast obliteration of funds which have withered on the vine, so to speak, for lack of pickers.

Anxiety over a possible dearth of funds overlooks the prevailing state of the economy. It also overlooks the essential character of the credit mechanism. Banks create funds in such a way as to pyramid prosperity. With their help business expansion in effect finances itself. Indeed, since this whole process depends on the continuation of general solvency and general confidence, the pyramiding process represents a very grave danger of sudden and calamitous collapse in time of crisis. Various controls have been proposed to deal with this threat to economic stability, running all the way from the mild discouragement which raising the Federal Reserve rediscount rate might bring to complete discontinuance of bank-created funds by the requirement of 'one hundred per cent reserves.'

This is one of the problems on which the adoption of limited capitalism would have little effect one way or the other. For if limited capitalism were to banish the fear of financial crisis and so encourage credit inflation, it would also check the impulse to runaway expansion by eliminating runaway 'prosperity.' It is regrettable, perhaps, that income diversion

would not solve all problems. But regret over the persistence of the credit problem should serve to allay any fears of
a dearth of funds under limited capitalism. Funds cannot
be simultaneously too many and too few. If credit expansion would still constitute a problem, that means that availability of funds would not.

There is one respect in which income diversion would
modify the financial pattern. Industrial expansion is financed,
not only by investing funds contributed by outside savers,
but also by 'plowing back' the earnings of the expanding
businesses themselves. Perhaps the clearest example of this
process is the Ford Motor Company. The only outside capital ever invested in this company was the twenty-eight
thousand dollars that was subscribed when the company was
first organized. Its entire subsequent growth has been
financed out of plowed-back earnings.

In recent years this source of capital funds has become
increasingly important. Many large corporations have thus
made themselves entirely, or largely, independent of the
money market. This practice has its good side. It is a form
of 'equity financing' in the sense that such accumulated
funds are owned outright, and consequently their use involves no increase of bonded indebtedness. Since bonded
indebtedness, like farmers' mortgages, has frequently led to
bankruptcy, such equity financing has the approval of business advisers. But it also has its bad side. This method of
financing is much more accessible to vast corporations
whose affairs contain more than a hint of monopoly power
than it is to young and small companies which are engaged
in a competitive struggle for survival. Indeed, the ability of
great corporations to finance themselves in this fashion is one
aspect of what has come to be known as 'security capital-

ism'; that is, a situation in which the effort to retain more or less exclusive control of certain markets and products has supplanted the competitive struggle to get more business by selling better products at lower prices.

Income diversion would undoubtedly reduce the ability of big business to finance itself in this manner. For to be successful any attempt to divert income from large-income channels would have to take account of the undivided earnings of such businesses. Not to do so would be to leave a broad avenue of escape for the very thing such an instrument as progressive taxation would seek to capture, namely, the increase of income of large income-receivers.

Such an avenue could easily be closed. A confiscatory tax on undivided surplus would do it, since it would present the owners of the business with a choice between paying personal income taxes on the earnings of their business or losing them altogether. The undivided surplus tax of 1936 did not do this, but it was sufficiently effective to raise an anguished outcry which led to its repeal by the next Congress.

However, to subject all business earnings to progressive income taxation would deprive the owners — to some degree, in proportion to the size of their incomes — of their ability to finance industrial growth out of earnings. Would it, therefore, reduce the ability of the economy to finance industrial growth? This has sometimes been claimed on the ground of what happens to those particular earnings.

But that claim has no validity. It is true, of course, that if those particular earnings were diverted from those particular large incomes to small-income channels, a greater part of the total flow of income would be spent in consumer purchases and a smaller part would be accumulated for investment.

Those particular income-receivers, who would otherwise be owners of equities in the equity-financed growth of their particular companies, would not have as much as formerly to reinvest. Would this mean a fatal deficiency of funds for the economy as a whole? To argue that it would is to ignore all the rest of the economy — to ignore all that we know about fund accumulation in general — and to assume that the condition of these few is necessarily the condition of all.

Income diversion in the amount necessary to maintain full production and full employment would not impair the ability of the economy to finance industrial growth. It would affect the financial pattern somewhat. For it would break the monopoly of big business over the financing of industrial growth and would give greater strength to small business. This would be true in so far as great corporations are controlled by people of large income and in so far as small businesses are owned by people with (relatively) small incomes. For if all business earnings were forced into the personal incomes of their owners, and if these were subjected to progressive taxation, the proportion taken in taxes would vary in direct ratio to the size of the incomes. Thus, the ability of the owners of small incomes and businesses to finance expansion out of earnings would be impaired much less than that of the owners of large incomes and businesses. Impairment, such as it is, would vary in direct ratio to the size of the income and, presumably, the business.

These obvious facts are in direct contradiction of the loudest outcry of the opponents of such taxation. Spokesmen of big business all agree that to force business earnings to undergo personal income taxation is to threaten small business with extinction. Their solicitude for small business is indeed touching. But it also strongly suggests the adroitest maneu-

ver of the supersalesman. The supersalesman invariably
singles out his product's chief defect to be the object of his
highest praise. That is what the outcry over undivided-sur-
plus taxation really means. Little business is the subject of
all the panegyrics. But the eulogists are the spokesmen of
big business, and they know where they hurt.

This effect of income diversion is incidental. But it should,
of course, be taken into account. It is a decentralizing
effect, and as such is desirable or not according to whether
it is desirable that the economy should be more monopolistic
or more competitive. To restore competition is not the
primary object of income diversion. Hence no extended discussion of the monopoly problem has been made a part of
the present discussion. That problem would still remain to
plague even limited capitalism. Indeed, limited capitalism
might find its legacy of monopoly its greatest and most insistent problem. But in so far as income diversion has any
effect on this situation, its effect is bound to be anti-monopo-
listic and pro-competitive.

The primary object of income diversion is the achievement and maintenance of full production. The fear has been
expressed, somewhat disingenuously, by spokesmen of large
income-receivers, that attainment of full production by such
a method would be at the expense of the fund-accumulating
that is necessary to industrial growth. That fear is wholly
without foundation. Our economy never has suffered from
over-all dearth of funds, and there is no indication that such
a thing is possible.

21

The Emoluments of Wealth

UNDER LIMITED CAPITALISM the rich would still be rich. This may seem regrettable to humanitarian idealists as well as to orthodox socialists. To such critics the question, 'Why should they?' seems unanswerable. But if it is, so is the counterquestion, 'Why shouldn't they?'

For if the rich have no right to be rich, neither have the poor. The greatest weakness of most of our thinking on this subject is that it retains for the poor what it denies to the rich.

The supposed rights of the 'upper classes' are, of course, spurious. They derive from the myth of feudal status and therefore have no standing in an enlightened and democratic world. Furthermore — so we commonly continue — all the emoluments of wealth are stolen from the poor. But what does this mean? However we may phrase it, the idea of theft clearly implies a prior right which has been violated. But how does it come about that the poor have all the rights? We may agree with the cynic who remarked that God must have loved the poor, since He made so many of them, but mere existence establishes no rights.

The ground on which the supposed rights of labor have usually been established is the supposed sacredness of toil. Work, it has been thought, establishes the right of the worker to the fruits of his own toil. But this is a very shaky argument. We must never forget Locke. He used this very argument as the basis of the rights of property. There is no biological, evolutionary, or historical ground for such a theory. Animals fight over the carcasses of their prey, but it would be ridiculous to build a theory of social organization on such a foundation. In certain instances primitive communities recognize what might be identified as rights of workmanship, but in many other instances they completely fail to do so. In many such communities much of the work of building houses, making nets for fishing, and so on, is a community enterprise. The participants in the effort establish no claims thereby. Where the women hoe the fields, they establish no rights in the resulting crops.

The truth is, the idea of rights is an eighteenth-century conception for which the twentieth century has no use. To impute the whole product of industry to labor is to do exactly what classical economic theory tried to do, with this difference that, whereas classical theory tried to show that each of the 'factors of production' gets what it deserves, the labor theory claims that the worker deserves all. The ground on which the claim is made is the same in both instances: desert. But what is desert? And who is 'the worker'? Surely not just the horny-handed. Engineers are just as indispensable to industrial society as stevedores, and even mathematicians — even, perhaps, poets.

This does not mean that whatever is, is just. There is no one among us who has not felt at some time that existing arrangements are unjust — that it is a scandal for stockbrokers to be rich while men who are later discovered to be great scientists and great artists live and die in obscurity and even poverty. In this state of mind it is the obscene antics of the rich that stink in our nostrils.

Certainly the ostentation of the rich is 'hard to take.' But while we are considering what to do about it there are two things we must be careful not to overlook. One is the importance of a starting-point. Regret over the fate of poets and scientists now dead is one thing, and responsibility for discovering the prospective great in early youth is quite another. Such being the case, perhaps it would be just as well to retain the garrets and the college professorships for a while. 'From each according to his ability; to each according to his need,' is a noble formula. But who knows our abilities, or needs, until they have been proved?

It is very much easier to deal with actually existing instances — to consider whether some particular person or class of persons needs all that he now gets, or whether someone else may not need more — than to start from scratch and try to do absolute justice without the guidance of any *status quo ante*. Consequently, we must realize that existing arrangements have the great merit of actuality.

In society as it actually exists the rich are rich, and the poor are poor, not because they deserve to be, but simply because they are. This does not mean they should be, or even that they will always continue to be, as rich or as poor as they are now. We might do well to demand of each that he should show cause why his condition should not be altered. But we, too, must be prepared to show cause why it should; and since this is a very considerable task, we may well be thankful that meantime an actuality for which we have no direct personal responsibility will continue to exist.

The second caution concerns the extravagances of the rich. On what ground can any cause be shown? Abilities and needs are significant not in relation to each 'individuality.' Such individuality is a metaphysical abstraction. The only basis for objective judgment is that afforded by the community. The question is, What does the poet, the scientist, or the stockbroker contribute to the life of the community?

When the extravagances of the rich are tested by this question, a paradox appears. However fantastic they may be, these extravagances are expenditures. As such they flow through the channels of consumer purchasing power and serve the important function of sustaining production and employment by absorbing the product of the industry.

To be sure, the 'conspicuous waste' of the idle rich is functionally different from, and economically inferior to, the mass consumption of the community at large. A million dollars spent by a million men will be expended upon staples and will constitute a fairly steady demand for a variety of basic products, whereas a million dollars squandered by one man is likely to take the form of highly sporadic demand for products of little permanent significance to the economy.

This is the answer to cynics like Mandeville who declared that 'private vices are public virtues,' and represented the antics of the rich as the mainstay of prosperity. They are not. But neither are they our greatest threat.

The greatest danger of great wealth is not what meets the eye and disgusts the decency of the casual observer. It is not the expenditures but the non-expenditures of wealth that threaten the stability of the economy. Society can easily afford the wildest extravagances of the rich. Our trouble is not that we cannot produce enough to go around, even around the rich. The serious trouble results from our failure to consume what we are well able to produce. What we cannot afford is the diversion of more funds from mass-consumer spending than the rich can either spend or invest. If we can prevent that from happening, we can afford to tolerate all the conspicuous waste in which the rich are able to indulge.

Such an arrangement will fail to satisfy utopians, and it may fail to satisfy some of the rich, for two reasons, one an individual matter and the other a matter of class.

Taxes are by tradition as inevitable as death. But business losses are not. They are matters of luck, or of individual acumen. Consequently, any individual of means might resent taxation the object of which is to prevent losses which he as an individual might confidently expect to avoid. Not everybody loses in a depression. But a depression can be avoided only if everybody is subjected to income limitation through progressive taxation.

In this situation many individuals would prefer to take their chances with depression. But society cannot permit individuals to take chances in situations in which society as a whole stands to lose. The case is identical with that of a threatened epidemic. Certain individuals, confident of their immunity to the disease, may resist being vaccinated. But society cannot permit them to gamble with the health of the community. No individual could possibly assume the responsibility for recompensing the community for the damage that might result from his losing his gamble with his own health or his own fortune. Consequently, his refusal to be guided by the requirements of the community is utterly irresponsible and cannot be tolerated.

The other ground for resentment by the rich is a matter of class. Under limited capitalism society could easily afford to tolerate individual wealth, but would no longer recognize any divine right to wealth or social position. To some people this would mean intolerable loss of 'face.'

For class consciousness always begins at the top. The only people to whom class is a real and vital thing are the people of class. In spite of all the assurances which limited capitalism extends, some people would no doubt regard it as only the first step toward total revolution. Some do so already. Progressive income taxation is still occasionally denounced as a sinister first step toward absolute equality.

This is, of course, the Bourbon state of mind. People who hold it are economic royalists in the most literal sense. That is, their attitude is identical with that of the adherents of James II and the principle of divine right of kings in England and with that of the French aristocrats who successfully resisted the Turgot reforms and so brought on the French Revolution.

If that state of mind prevails among the rich and powerful members of our community, it will make total revolution inevitable here and now as it would have done in England in 1688, and actually did in France in 1789. Whether it does so or not depends in part upon events. A sudden, violent, and prolonged depression might arouse exasperation on both sides of the social conflict so extreme as to make any compromise with total revolution quite impossible. But it also depends in part upon the persuasiveness of a reasonable compromise. Limited monarchy offered such a possibility in England in 1688, and that alternative prevailed. No such alternative was clearly enough visualized in France in the years preceding the French Revolution to determine the outcome of that crisis.

Will limited capitalism forestall total revolution in America? That remains to be seen. It is a compromise under which individual wealth might continue to be tolerated. For industrial society could easily afford to support the rich in the manner to which, for whatever reason, they have become accustomed. But it could do so only by placing certain limitations on their incomes. These limitations would do nobody any real financial harm. But they would be offensive to the traditions of economic royalists. It is for the rich to decide whether they prefer to remain rich subject to the tolerance of the community, or to go to the guillotine as true-blue, die-hard advocates of the divine right of capital.

22

The Incentive to Create

T HE OBJECT of the rectification of the flow of income which has been proposed in this book is full production, the largest possible measure of employment, and the largest national income which the present attainments of science and the industrial arts are capable of producing. It has been pointed out repeatedly in the preceding chapters and is a commonplace of present-day economic thinking that the measures which are necessary to bring all this to pass do not involve any reduction of the realized incomes and actual expenditures either of the large number of people who are in moderately comfortable circumstances or of the handful of the rich.

Nothing has been said about equalization, nor has any tendency in this direction been tactfully concealed. To the minds of some readers this may be a fault. Equality is a noble word, certainly no less so than freedom. The idea of equality is deeply embedded in the Christian tradition and in the American tradition. There is scarcely anyone who has not sometimes reflected upon the travesties of inequality. Why should movie actors and actresses of doubtful abilities

146

(whatever may be their physical endowments) and still more doubtful character receive many times as much as any of the world's greatest scientists or scholars? Why should a dealer make millions out of the works of artists who died in penury?

It is to be hoped that an advancing civilization will some day learn to deal with questions such as these. The present discussion has made no attempt to do so, for obvious reasons. Our concern has not been with the ultimate perfection of the race, but with imminent disaster. Even if we succeed in warding off the disaster to the brink of which capitalism has brought us, we shall still be far from utopia. But we shall at least be extant. The further improvement of our lot will at least not be impeded by that circumstance.

Meantime there are others — they are unlikely to be readers of this book! — who affect to see the cloven hoof of equalitarianism beneath the haircloth of every proposal for reform. One still encounters people, otherwise sane and literate, who insist that the very principle of direct progressive taxation can have no other object than eventual equality. In denouncing such an outcome as devilish, in spite of our religious and political ideals, they insist that Nature itself breeds inequality, and so that any attempt to reduce all men to a common level must inevitably be a Procrustean abomination. It is hard to see how taking four per cent of a thousand dollars and ninety per cent of a million dollars will reduce the subjects of progressive taxation to dull equality. But the denunciation of the flat equalization of all incomes is not without a measure of justification.

Nature does breed inequality. According to the biologists, this is fortunate, since it means that some few are far superior to the common run. Furthermore, the Christian belief is that all men are equal in the eyes of God, but men are not expected to view each other in divine perspective. Similarly, all men are equal in the eyes of the law, but not equally guilty or equally stupid.

Even the needs of different men are very different. Reactionaries make a great to-do over their discovery of inequalities among idealists. But the truth is, idealists are not all as fatuous as they are supposed to be. Plato proposed to recognize major inequalities in his ideal republic, and the watchword of modern socialism, 'to each according to his need,' is clearly incompatible with flat equality. This has been recognized both in theory and in practice by most socialists — certainly by Karl Marx and by his followers in the Soviet Union. Even the tiny utopian communities, where the nearest approach to a common standard of living has been achieved, nevertheless recognize that leaders incur extraordinary expenses which the communities do not hesitate to defray. And so do mothers. Furthermore, the simplicity of such communities is a function of their size. In the great society differences of occupation are correspondingly wide, with consequent differences of need. These differences go far beyond the specific requirements of formal education and the like. Even the needs of temperament are very real and considerable. 'Idea men' need relaxation, refreshment, and even stimulation; and all this is no less true of industry than of science and the arts.

People who insist that a very considerable measure of inequality is the inevitable accompaniment of a complex society are quite right. The important thing is to be honest about it. The fact that Nature breeds inequality does not prevent scientists from deploring the reproduction of congenital idiots. Wagner's affectations may have been justified by his music dramas (though his old friend Nietzsche thought otherwise). But what is the justification of the extravagances of the playboys who compose no music, write no poetry, and assume no responsibility whatever for the conduct of the industries from which they derive their royal perquisites? Are we to conclude that since inequality is a law of nature and of society, therefore no line can be drawn between what is sound and what is perverse?

Should we go further and welcome the perverse? Is the perversity of his descendants the necessary incentive by which alone the captain of industry is induced to put forth his creative efforts? Perhaps this question is prejudiced. Doubtless no one who founds a fortune and a dynasty can foresee all the consequences of his acts. Very likely such a person is moved by immediate and purely quantitative considerations. But if it is true that only the prospect of unlimited gains will move businessmen to put forth their greatest efforts, then it may be true that any curtailment of that prospect may have the effect of dampening their ardor. Such a claim is frequently made, and it is one that must be met. If the community is indeed beholden to captains of industry for their organizing genius, and if the full measure of that genius can be realized — to the advantage of the whole community — only when it is inspired by the prospect of unlimited gains, then any limitation upon large incomes may do more harm than good.

In considering this claim, we should first of all recall Thorstein Veblen's dictum that the gains of business enterprisers are proportional, not to the magnitude of their creative achievements, but 'to the magnitude of the disturbances they are able to create.' Applied to all business activities, this is of course a prodigious overstatement. But it con-

tains a kernel of truth that is of utmost importance. Great
fortunes have been founded upon earthquakes and tidal
waves by the simple expedient of buying up the victims'
property at distress values. As every businessman knows,
fortunes can be made out of financial panics by the simple
expedient of selling short. And whereas earthquakes and
tidal waves are beyond our power to create, financial panics
are not. To create a disturbance of some sort with a view
to making other people dump their property on the market
at sacrifice values is one of the standard formulas of business
strategy.

But what goes on here? There are two types of business
activity. One consists in organizing a productive enterprise
of some sort. The other consists in taking some other person's enterprise away from him. In the career of any given
businessman, these two types of activity may both be represented. But that does not prevent our making a distinction
between them and even inquiring whether both respond
equally to the same incentives. Is it true that no businessman will bother to organize and conduct any productive
activity unless it offers the prospects of unlimited gains? If
so, then everything the economists have said about competition is totally false; for the very essence of competition is
the choice between a more profitable and a less profitable
venture, the presumption being that the more profitable one
will be chosen quite irrespective of the absolute magnitude
of the expected gains.

Predatory activities might indeed be affected by a limitation upon gains. They might be affected — adversely, as it
were — by a resolute program of income taxation. But in
that case we may as well be perfectly clear about it. A limitation upon gains will indeed discourage one type of busi-

ness activity. That type is not creative, and is no advantage whatever to anybody but the successful buccaneer and his descendants. Indeed, in so far as the buccaneer creates (or aggravates) disturbances so as to increase the scope of his piratical activities, he does so to the detriment of the community. It is this activity alone the incentive to which might be diminished by such measures as progressive income taxation.

In recent years there has been much talk of 'venture capital.' The idea is that some undertakings are peculiarly risky. This is especially true, so it seems, of undertakings in new fields. At the same time, these are the very undertakings by which the life of the community may be enriched and even perhaps its experience enlarged. Therefore, it is important to the community that such undertakings should be encouraged, and the only effective encouragement is the prospect of unusually large gains — large enough, indeed, to offset the unusual risks involved. Any limitation upon prospective gains, such as high progressive taxation, would, it is said, diminish this prospect to the point at which businessmen would decline to take such risks, to the great loss of the community.

But in the discussion of such ventures two quite distinct considerations are sadly confused. One is the judgment of the businessman upon an actual venture in which he may be interested. The other is blackmail.

Because many new ventures fail, and because the public knows no more about any one than any other, we therefore conclude that businessmen are in the same case, and think of them as gamblers betting blindly on the turn of a card. But in fact no businessman ever enters upon any venture in such a spirit. He 'takes a chance' only after investigation has convinced him that he holds winning cards. This is true, notwithstanding the contrary judgment of other businessmen who may have investigated the same project. So far as he can know anything, this businessman knows that such a venture represents Fate knocking at his door. What must Fate offer him in the way of reward before he will consent to open the door? Once again, we must remember the competitive principle. All that is necessary to induce a businessman to embark on such a venture is the prospect of greater gains than he can realize elsewhere. To suppose that a businessman will refuse to go into an undertaking, which to his certain knowledge promises to be more profitable than other undertakings accessible to him, unless the prospect is infinite is to suppose either that the competitive principle is without force or that businessmen are utter fools.

It is true that businessmen do sometimes decline, or at least postpone, reasonably profitable opportunities, opportunities which they might have been expected on purely competitive considerations to have taken. Why do they do so? If we are to believe their public utterances, it is because they are discouraged. The prospect of profit, so they say, is not enough to stimulate their flagging spirits. This declaration clearly implies the possibility of change, the possibility, for example, that taxes which their possible earnings would now incur might at some future time be reduced, to their eventual and permanent advantage. Such being the case, their declaration is plain blackmail. In effect, they are saying to the community, 'Here is a new industry. I am convinced that it has a great future. Its creation will be advantageous to you. But I will not go into it unless you will sweeten the kitty.'

There are two things that can be done in such a situation. One is to give in, with all the consequences which must sooner or later attend the continued maldistribution of income. The other is to make it quite clear that we do not propose to be blackmailed. We have absolutely nothing to lose by the latter course. No businessman should ever be encouraged to embark on any enterprise unless he is convinced that it is going to pay. If he is convinced that a given prospect will pay, and if he is also convinced that he has nothing to gain by waiting for a change of political administrations, ordinary competitive gains are quite sufficient to bring him into action.

For we are not advocating the abolition of all gains. Such a rectification of the flow of income as is necessary to preserve the industrial economy from utter disaster would still leave great inequalities of income. As we have noted repeatedly, our economy can easily afford even the wildest extravagances of expenditure on the part of the very rich. It can and doubtless will always continue to produce new fortunes. Sheer chance still plays a tremendous part in human affairs and doubtless will do so always. No change in the flow of income will prevent the features of a new actress from catching the public fancy, nor will it prevent people from getting rich as the result of the discovery (by others, perhaps) of hitherto unknown minerals underneath their stony and unprofitable pastures.

Nor will it discourage anybody from doing what is the most profitable and agreeable thing for him to do in any case. For we must never forget that to people of executive temperament management is agreeable, just as acting is agreeable to the histrionically disposed and writing poetry is agreeable to poets. It may be that a more orderly world would discourage buccaneering to some degree, but that is a contingency which we could learn to bear. The world is trying to discourage national aggression, but nobody supposes that the end of aggression would mean the end of civilized government. To suppose that the discouragement of financial piracy, to whatever slight degree, would be at the expense of industrial growth is no more sensible.

23

Economic Freedom

'F REE PRIVATE ENTERPRISE' is the most effective phrase that could possibly be chosen to extol the virtues of capitalism. These are noble words. Freedom, surely, is one of the noblest in the language, privacy one of the most precious, and enterprise one of the most admirable. Such words sum up the aspirations by which the Western peoples have been chiefly stirred for some hundreds of years. To speak of free private enterprise is to invoke ideals for which our fore-fathers have fought and by which their children have been inspired generation after generation.

Meantime the phrase 'free private enterprise' has taken on another meaning. In recent decades this phrase has come into quite general use to refer to a certain type of public policy, namely, the opposite of 'government interference.' Any sort of government curb on any sort of business has come to be understood as an infringement of 'free private enterprise.' This is true even of the antitrust laws and their enforcement.

Doubtless there is some verbal justification for the use of the phrase 'free private enterprise' in this connection. Business, even the biggest business, is commonly regarded as 'private' as distinguished from government, which is 'public.' Consequently, any governmental restraint upon any business activity is an infringement of the 'freedom' of a 'private enterprise.' But when the phrase is used in this sense, it does not necessarily retain any of the nobility which attaches to the historic ideals of freedom and privacy. It was not for the freedom or privacy of great corporations that our forefathers once fought. To assume that it was — to use the phrase 'free private enterprise' as though its two meanings were identical and inseparable — is to commit a hoax.

The common belief that all economic freedom begins and ends with capitalism rests on nothing but this hoax. Indeed, it is a double hoax. Not only are the two meanings of the phrase 'free private enterprise' entirely distinct; any attempt to trace a historical connection between them can succeed only by committing a second hoax on history.

The history of capitalism falls into two periods, that of mercantilism and that of *laissez faire*. During the mercantilist period a few great trading companies flourished mightily, in large measure as a result of the special privileges they were able to exact from their royal sovereigns. Small-businessmen who tried to 'muscle in' on the 'rackets' of the great trading companies were known as 'interlopers,' and the supreme coercive power of the state was liberally used to keep them out.

The transition from mercantilism to *laissez faire* was not only one of economic change; the economic function and even the essential character of government changed quite as much as the economic situation. The triumph of parliamentary democracy over royal prerogative meant the triumph of the business community at large over their dynastic sovereigns and at the same time over the great companies to which those sovereigns had granted special privileges.

It was this situation which gave its original meaning to the phrase, *laissez faire*. Hitherto the principal economic function of (dynastic) government had been the issuance and maintenance of monopolistic privilege. What *laissez faire* denounced was that kind of government performing that kind of function, and what it called for was the cessation of that kind of business and the extinction of that kind of government.

'Free private enterprise' is a modern phrase. But the feelings aroused by important historical situations have a way of lingering long after the actual situations which produced them have passed away. Such are the feelings which the phrase 'free private enterprise' still conjures up. We are still denouncing the tyrant, George III, and his vicious Navigation Acts, and our vehement sincerity expresses our conviction still that our position in this matter has been just and right.

But meantime the situation has changed again. Small business triumphed over big business in the eighteenth century, but meantime big business has again put in its appearance. Today it dominates the economic scene more than ever before. But government is now on the other side. This is true, of course, only with reservations. Big business still seeks and obtains from government special privileges of all sorts. But that is not what people have in mind when they denounce present-day government for its meddlesomeness. What they mean to denounce is the attempt of government to check, restrain, and control big business. It is these efforts which now constitute 'unwarrantable interference' with free private enterprise.

In short, the present application of the phrase 'free private enterprise' is the exact opposite of the one by which it was established so firmly in our hearts. The cry of economic freedom was first raised when the chief economic function of government was to grant patents of monopoly. Now government is our only hope of controlling private monopoly, and it is in contravention of this hope that the old cry is now raised. If anyone doubts this, let him note who the people are that raise the cry. They are not the little men, the economically underprivileged, the forgotten men. 'Free private enterprise' is not the rallying cry of revolutionaries. It is the gospel of the National Association of Manufacturers and the United States Chamber of Commerce.

Is real economic freedom the freedom of every man to find employment for his talents? Is it the freedom of common citizens to conduct their private lives in the manner to which industrial civilization has become accustomed? Or is it the freedom of the economically powerful to dominate the economically weak? There can be no question about the freedom for which our forefathers once fought. It was the freedom of serfs from feudal bondage, the freedom of subjects to be citizens, their freedom not to be taxed except by themselves.

Two sets of circumstances contributed to secure such freedom and such privacy. One is the development of science and technology throughout modern times, and perhaps even in ancient times. Freedom of purchase and sale are conditioned by freedom of intercourse and freedom of movement. This whole dependence is summed up by economists in the word 'mobility.' Perfect competition, we say, assumes complete mobility. That is, it assumes that people know what is going on elsewhere and are able to go there without hin-

drance. But how can they know, and how can they go?
Knowing and going mean more than the absence of legal
prohibitions. To know anything in the human sense is a
function of language. To put spoken words in writing vastly
extends the function of knowing. That is why the invention
of writing is one of the great landmarks of human progress,
and that is why the invention of printing (by movable types,
in the European manner) is another landmark of corresponding moment. More than to any law or institution, economic
or political, we owe the general condition which made the
'free' market possible to the invention of printing.

But developments in transportation were of like importance. Mobility is a matter of transport. We call the nine-
teenth century the railway age, and rightly so; and we look
forward to the twenty-first, or even perhaps the latter half
of the twentieth, for the dawn of the air age. But in a no
less significant sense the preceding period was the age of
ships; and even before ships had been developed that were
capable of carrying Europeans to the shores of other continents — even before medieval civilization had reached its
apogee — there occurred in western Europe a revolution in
harness, horse-drawn vehicles, and road-making.

It is to circumstances such as these that we owe the melt-
ing of the feudal system and the social fluidity of which the
free market is a consequence. The most important freedom,
certainly, is freedom of the mind. But, as we have begun
to learn, the mind is not an altogether separate thing. The
circumstances which have shaped our lives have also shaped
our minds, and vice versa. The advancement of science and
the spread of general enlightenment are effects as well as
causes of the development of the instruments of communication and transport. The mobility which conditions the

free market is in part a matter of venturesomeness; and venturesomeness is itself a consequence of getting around. Freedom, we often say, is in the heart — meaning the mind. But the mentality of freedom and the physical instrumentalities of movement and communication are obverse and reverse of the one thing: modern man.

Would this freedom be endangered by any departure from absolute capitalism? Before trying to answer this question, we must first recognize that there is a sense in which freedom is embodied in the institutional structure of society. Here is the other set of circumstances by which freedom and privacy have been secured. The runaway serfs who found haven in the medieval towns and formed the nucleus of the middle class which was eventually to set the pattern of Western society could not have found any such haven if the march of industrial progress even at that early day had not brought roads and vehicles and river barges to give them occupations; and they could not have maintained their rights of asylum without the bulwark of legal institutions.

Among the legal and political institutions by which the freedom of the common man was safeguarded was the institution of property. In that early day it was his legal version of the noble's castle. This is still an attribute of the institution of property. The plain man's security from violent entry and seizure is still an aspect of the rights of property. But nothing ever stands still, not even social institutions. The functions of an institution change. That is why the price of freedom is eternal vigilance: vigilance for the changed circumstances that alter cases.

For the institution of property also covers rights to income. As property has grown in magnitude, the income pat-

terns it determines have seriously affected the freedom of
the common man. Economists have always realized that
economic freedom is qualified by lack of means. This is true
both of freedom of purchase and of freedom of occupation.
We sometimes speak of the operation of economic demand
as a democratic system, since every purchase is a vote by
which the productive resources of the community are ulti-
mately allocated. But this is a system of balloting in which
one man casts dollar ballots while another casts million-
dollar ballots. How undemocratic this is would be instantly
apparent if it were proposed that political ballots be distributed according to incomes. The poor man is free to
spend his pittance as best he can. If he is unemployed, he
is free to starve, and, as Scrooge remarked on that celebrated Christmas Eve, 'decrease the surplus population.'

In the same fashion a poor man is free to take up any
occupation which his means permit. By attending a university for eight years or more he may become a doctor or a
lawyer or an engineer. Or, if he has the means, he can establish himself in the aluminum business or the telephone business or the glass-bottle business or the shoe-machine business in competition with certain well-known firms which are
now engaged in these undertakings.

Obviously, our freedom is far from perfect now, and the
question is: Do we owe such freedom as we have to capitalism? Would we lose even this measure of freedom — very
considerable as compared with feudalism and therefore correspondingly precious — if capitalism were to suffer any
change? We might, if the change were total. Doubtless the
police state would be a change for the worse. But limited
capitalism certainly would not. The whole object of limited
capitalism is to give greater scope to the industrial process

through which freedom grows. It would do this precisely by correcting those discrepancies in the flow of income by which freedom is now most constrained; and it would do this without any modification of the basic rights of property which constitute the sole ground for the historic identification of capitalism with economic freedom.

Those who oppose such changes in the name of 'free private enterprise' are committing the great hoax. They mean by free private enterprise the freedom of the strong to dominate the weak without 'government interference.' If that is not what they mean, let them make it clear by a plain declaration on the subject of big business. Do they in fact renounce monopoly? Can they give us any assurance of their sincerity in this regard? That is the acid test of their sincerity — or duplicity.

If they are smart, the spokesmen of big business will stop pretending that free private enterprise means freedom for them and will do their best to enlarge our common freedom. For private owners will continue to exercise discretionary control over their businesses only if the present structure of society is preserved more or less intact. This can be done only if the industrial economy can be made to work, and the industrial economy can be made to work only if consumption can be brought into line with production. That could be accomplished by a diversion of income which would leave the present structure of society virtually intact. It would be capitalism still, but limited capitalism. Consequently, nobody has a greater stake in limited capitalism than the present loud advocates of free private enterprise. For the only alternative is a far more drastic modification of the social structure on which private ownership itself depends.

24

The Demon State

Dᴜʀɪɴɢ ᴛʜᴇ ʟᴀsᴛ ғᴇᴡ ʏᴇᴀʀs wide currency has been given
to a very disturbing idea. The idea is that all attempts to
modify the ideas and institutions of absolute capitalism,
whatever their character and however fine the motives of
their originators, must inevitably lead toward totalitarian
dictatorship.

This idea is a sincere expression of classical liberalism.
As such it is an example of the persistence of ancient sentiments to which reference was made in the last chapter. Because governments once nourished mercantilist monopoly,
the early advocates of free competition were moved to declare that the best government is the least government —
that the 'automatic adjustment' of all economic activity by
'the impersonal forces of supply and demand' should be as
free as possible from governmental 'interference.' Those
who fear what they call 'statism' today boast that their ideas
derive from this eighteenth-century situation. Ignoring all
the present connotations of the word 'liberal,' they declare
themselves to be the only true liberals in the 'original' sense
of that long-suffering term.

Obviously, a great deal turns on the qualification, 'as free as possible.' No one has ever advocated complete freedom. Indeed, it is doubtful if that phrase has any meaning, since capitalism itself rests on private property, and private property assumes that title to property is governmentally determined and assured. Moreover, all economists recognize that governmental responsibility changes with changing technology. Very few traffic regulations were necessary in the eighteenth century, but nobody would care to operate twentieth-century vehicles with eighteenth-century 'freedom.' Even time was free from governmental interference in the eighteenth century. 'Standard time' was adopted by law in the United States only about 1883, and at the insistence of the railroads.

No one could possibly deny that our need for governmental regulation is very different when 'you can reach any place on earth from your home airport in sixty hours' from what it was when Adam Smith toured Europe in a coach-and-four. Consequently, sweeping denunciations of governmental action would receive very little credence today, in spite of ancient sentiment, except for two things. One is the dread spectacle of totalitarian dictatorship, and the other is the recent plethora of governmental regulations.

These two things, occurring together, have been profoundly disturbing. Are they indeed cause and effect? That is what the 'true liberals' say. In substance they say, 'You see what is happening in Europe, and you see what is happening in this country. You don't like what is happening in Europe. But what is happening in this country is only a way-station on the road to what is happening in Europe. That is how it happened in Europe. These dictatorships began, as we are beginning, with a vast increase of governmental regulation. That is what led to dictatorship there, and it will inevitably do the same here, if we continue as we are doing now.'

Is this true? The facts are plain and obdurate. Totalitarianism over there and greatly increased regulation here are both facts. Their simultaneity is another very disturbing fact. It would be quite implausible, under the circumstances, to deny that there is any connection. But there might be another connection. Instead of totalitarianism being the result of which regulation is the cause, both might conceivably be results of something else. Surely it would be only the most elementary logical precaution for us to inquire whether any third condition may perhaps exist of which both of these may be results.

If we make such an inquiry, we can scarcely avoid getting a positive answer. There is indeed a third condition whose relation to the other two is too close to admit of argument. We can call it the crisis of capitalism, or world economic prostration, or just depression, according to our lights. But no one can deny that such a condition has existed or that it has prevailed in each of the regions under consideration.

This leads to the question, What is the relation between this economic prostration and the two conditions with which we are concerned, totalitarianism and regulation? Is it conceivable that both of these conditions may be results of economic prostration? Here again the answer is inescapable. Not only is such a thing conceivable; precisely that has been the prevailing explanation of both of these conditions all along.

For every writer who attributes the rise of totalitarianism to abandonment of *laissez faire* in favor of progressive regulation there are a hundred who have attributed it to the dis-

orders which have attended economic prostration. And the
same is true of regulation. It is, of course, true that the kind
of regulation which eighteenth-century liberals fear is not
exemplified by time standardization and traffic control. It is
rather securities-and-exchange regulation, monetary regulation, holding-company regulation, wage-and-hour regulation, 'pump-priming,' 'made work,' agricultural 'adjustment,'
and all that sort of thing. But all these measures have one
thing, and only one, in common. All were undertaken in the
effort to overcome economic prostration.

Such being the case, it does not by any means follow that
the regulations in question necessarily lead to dictatorship.
The truth may be the exact opposite. It may well be that
countries which have enacted regulations such as these have
thereby achieved, if not a final and complete solution of
their problems, at least sufficient relief from economic prostration to escape the fate into which other countries have
been thrust by their failure (or their inability, for whatever
reason) to follow such a course.

To recognize the possibility of this interpretation of the
facts is not to establish its truth. Nor is truth established by
majority vote. The very large number of economists, historians, and others who hold some such view as this does not
guarantee the correctness of their views. The 'true liberals'
may be right, nevertheless. But the crucial importance for
the whole argument of what, more than twenty-five years
ago, R. H. Tawney called 'the sickness of acquisitive society,'
coupled with the universality of the presumption that some
such condition does indeed exist (by whatever name it may
be called): these considerations do place a grave responsibility on anyone who proposes to discuss these matters. He
must take account of the fact that capitalism has been ail-

ing, or at least of the fact that a great many people have thought so. To ignore the problem altogether is, to say the least, very strange procedure on the part of presumably responsible scholars.

That is what these writers have done. Readers who find this hard to believe are invited to verify the matter for themselves. By far the most widely distributed, and therefore the most influential, of these pronouncements is *The Road to Serfdom,* by F. A. Hayek. Let any reader who has not already done so go through that book with this question in mind: 'To what extent does this book make its readers aware of the existence of any serious economic problems (other than state interference), or of the existence of any general belief to that effect on the part of responsible and informed students of these matters?' He will be amazed by what he finds. Not only does the book contain no hint of any sort of crisis in the affairs of capitalism, real or supposed; it gives the impression throughout that capitalism (or the economy of free private enterprise) is wholly free from any sort of fault or flaw. Even monopoly, which was the chief object of attack by the founders of *laissez-faire* economics and is still regarded by nearly all economists as a very serious problem, is brushed aside with the remark that 'the extent of the phenomenon is often greatly exaggerated,' and anyhow government, not business, is to blame for the 'suppression of competition' which has occurred.

The whole argument of the 'true liberals' rests on this omission. They do not refute the views of other scholars; they simply ignore them. They do not give another explanation of the troubles of capitalism; they simply ignore them. In effect they say: 'If you will concede that no reason exists for the regulatory efforts of modern governments or for the emergence of the modern dictators save the itch for power, then we will undertake to convince you that the itch for power is common to all governments and that its partial gratification is very dangerous since it is a step toward its total gratification.' In the absence of any other reason for any governmental activity, this is a convincing argument. But would anybody who is not in the grip of a fixed idea concede the major premise of such an argument?

The enormity of this omission is not limited to the identification of all regulatory efforts with incipient totalitarianism, which it thus makes possible. It also leads to the contemptuous dismissal of democracy.

There are two opposing views of democracy, both of which are well illustrated by conflicting interpretations of recent political events. According to one interpretation what is proved by the last four presidential elections is the folly of the electorate, its susceptibility to demagoguery — to charm of personality, to an effective radio delivery, and to astute political trickery. According to the other interpretation what is proved is that the people know where they hurt and want something vigorous done about it. On this theory it is held that the people were presented with sharply contrasting alternatives, especially in 1932. On one side was the stout denial that anything was amiss and the (somewhat contradictory) refusal to admit governmental responsibility for what was amiss; on the other was the clear recognition of the extreme gravity of the situation and the explicit promise of vigorous efforts to cope with it. According to this interpretation the people understood these alternatives and knowingly chose the latter.

As this case shows, the difference between these two interpretations of democracy turns on the reality, or unreality, of trouble. If there was no trouble in 1932 — if prosperity was 'just around the corner' regardless of who was elected president or what he might subsequently do — then, of course, it is impossible to credit democracy with having worked. And the opposite is also true. For if we were truly in desperate trouble, then it is likewise impossible to deny that awareness of that trouble affected the decision.

The same is true on a larger scale. 'True liberals' abhor government. They do so because they see nothing in politics but a struggle for power on the part of politicians. They see in democracy only a somewhat different kind of struggle from that of other days, one in which politicians 'compete' for the favors of an imbecile electorate by trying to outdo one another in lying cajolery and subtle corruption. That is why, so Hayek says, 'the worst get on top.'

Once again, if any reader doubts this, let him re-read *The Road to Serfdom* with the specific purpose of noting what its author thinks about democracy. A casual first reader could easily have missed this. Writers like Hayek are very eloquent on the subject of freedom; and since most Americans associate freedom with democracy, they would naturally suppose that Hayek does so too. But that is definitely not the case. 'True liberals' like Hayek define freedom as absence of government, even democratic government, or most of all democratic government, since it is in democracies that politicians get to the top by making utopian promises of full employment, freedom from want, a chicken in every pot and two cars in every garage — promises which commit them to acts of interfering folly, which must then be followed by repressive violence — and so on to Buchenwald.

On such assumptions, needless to say, limited capitalism

is an illusion. So is limited monarchy, and for the same reason. If there was nothing wrong in 1688, then all that happened was that a gang of Protestant politicians made an issue of King James's religion in order to seize the power for themselves. If there was nothing wrong with Germany but the follies of democracy, then Hitler must have been nourished on those follies.

But if something has been wrong — with feudalism, with absolute monarchy, and with absolute capitalism — then another interpretation must prevail. Then democracy is something more than demagoguery, then the revolution of 1688 was something more than a change of rascals, and then limited capitalism may indeed be the alternative to total revolution.

This whole discussion has been based on the fact of trouble. It began by showing why trouble was implicit in the basic ideas and institutions of absolute capitalism and how that trouble heads up in recurrent depression, war, and revolution. It has also been based on the conviction that democracy is a function of enlightenment. Enlightenment is never absolute, always partial. 'You can fool some of the people all of the time.' Enlightenment also comes slowly, and meantime accidents do happen. 'You can fool all of the people some of the time.' Nevertheless, enlightenment steadily increases. The careers of recent dictators have been startling enough, but more impressive has been the eventual arousal of the free peoples of the world and their demonstration of the power of understanding. 'You can't fool all of the people all of the time.'

All civilization, perhaps, is a race between disaster and enlightenment. No one could assert that in this race enlightenment is always ahead. But it is likewise true that enlightenment is still in the running. The disasters toward which industrial society has been traveling are indeed prodigious. But they are beginning to be quite generally understood, and it is still too early to count democracy out. Obviously, this book has been written in the conviction that intelligent modification of the existing social structure is still a possibility.

That possibility can be realized only by intelligently concerted action, one of the principal instruments of which is government. For government is not necessarily, by its essential nature, demoniacal. Government is what we make it. In spite of fools and demagogues we can make it an instrument of enlightenment, of the people, by the people, for the people. To propose to do so is indeed a high aspiration. It is not therefore naïve. The truly naïve are those who can see nothing in the past but failure and nothing in our present aspirations but egregious folly. Their cynicism is the state of mind that brings forth dictators, and it is the full measure of their folly that they are sincerely unaware of that enormity.

25

The Problem of Power

LIMITED CAPITALISM would bring no loss of freedom, economic or political. But the sinister fact of economic power would still remain. Very great concentration of ownership already exists, and still greater concentration of financial control; and this concentration of power would not be directly affected by measures explicitly designed to rectify the flow of income without any further modification of the present pattern of ownership and management.

In the minds of some critics of the whole 'underconsumptionist' way of thinking, this is a fatal defect. They denounce such measures on two grounds. The first is that of power. Financial power, they point out, is power over prices; and power over prices is power to divert income. This power could and presumably would be used to nullify any attempted diversion of income from large incomes to small incomes such as has been advocated in this book. Furthermore, they say, monopoly power has steadily increased throughout the century and a half during which competition has been our economic ideal and monopoly the epitome of evil, and it has done so because the monopolists have been able to withstand all attacks. Such being the case it is fatuous to suppose that they would now consent to the enactment of measures intended to deprive them of the fruits of their hard-won power.

These are practical considerations. But, say the critics, our theoretical shortcomings are no less damning. For, they say, the flow of income is determined by the basic institutional patterns of society. However income flows, it is symptomatic of that underlying condition and is determined by it. Consequently, in seeking to superimpose upon that underlying pattern some device or devices for rectifying the flow of income as it has already been determined by the basic institutions of society, we are proposing to treat the symptoms of what we ourselves regard as a deepseated, chronic, constitutional disease.

These criticisms faithfully reflect the views both of orthodox economists and of orthodox socialists. Both groups seek to confine the discussion to existing institutions, and both oppose the modification of existing institutions, the former because they believe that existing institutions are fundamentally sound and the latter because they believe existing institutions are completely rotten. If either of these judgments is correct, then the whole 'underconsumptionist' approach to the economic problem is misguided and the supposition that the flow of income can be successfully rectified is indeed fatuous.

But that is a very large 'if,' the contrary of which is also true. If the existing social order is neither absolutely rotten nor completely sound, then — extremists to the contrary notwithstanding — the problem is that of modifying existing institutions.

Such a modification is not necessarily superficial or ineffective simply by virtue of being a modification. All changes are more or less superficial and more or less fundamental according to the character of each particular change. If we define those institutions as fundamental which determine the flow of income, then a proposed institution which would substantially alter the flow of income is by the same definition just as fundamental as those previously so identified. This point was clearly recognized by a commission of economists who were assembled early in the Great Depression to diagnose our troubles and prescribe for them. One of the committees of this group summed up their judgment of what was wrong in the phrase, 'absence of essential institutions.' Our economy, they held, was not altogether in ruins; but it does lack some sort of stabilizing mechanism the action of which, like that of an automatic governor, would be of such vital importance for the whole as to justify calling it an essential institution.

The whole object of the way of thinking of which the present discussion is representative has been to supply that deficiency. It is true that doing so would, in a certain sense, 'make capitalism work.' This would be highly unpalatable to orthodox socialists, to whom capitalism is always capitalism and cannot change its spots. It would also be unpalatable to orthodox adherents of absolute capitalism, to whom limited capitalism may seem utterly communistic. In that case we should invite these critics to get together. The difference between absolute and limited capitalism can scarcely be utterly superficial and horrendously radical, both at the same time.

This dilemma grows out of a misconception of the nature of power. If income is the fruit of power, then any device which leaves financial power unchanged is by definition superficial and is virtually certain to prove ineffective in practice. But is income only a manifestation of power? That is how we have been accustomed to consider it. In all our social thinking — perhaps as a result of our preoccupation with war and the politics of which war is thought to be only an extension — considerations of power have indeed been paramount. Hence orthodox economists have conceived economic life as a struggle of each against all subject only to the 'natural laws' of supply and demand, and hence orthodox socialists have conceived it as a struggle between classes subject only to the similarly 'natural' law of dialectical materialism.

But is power the whole story? Or is coercive power — economic, political, familial, racial, tribal, theocratic, or otherwise — only one side of a picture which has another side that is quite different? We are beginning to see that such is actually the case. Indeed, the whole way of thinking which has found expression in this book may be said to be moving in precisely that direction: that is, toward the recognition of the reverse side of the social picture.

On one side, society is a power system. On the other, it is a tool system. Neither can exist alone. Each conditions the other. Neither is paramount. The fruits of power are also the fruits of industry. If power is exercised in such a way as to cripple industry, its fruit is thereby diminished. That is what the whole story has been about: the blighting of the industrial crop which results from the operation of the financial power system.

The fact that financial vested interests have the power to prevent the correction of this evil is quite irrelevant to the present argument. All power is power to commit suicide, and all forms of power are sometimes used to this effect. In

every situation there are always some who, through stupidity
or a pathological obstinacy, insist on rule-or-ruin. There are
also some who are prepared to gamble on their personal immunity to a general disaster. But are these the motives by
which our opposition is inspired?

Certainly the motives of monopoly capitalism are very
different. Those who control vast empires are apt to move
with corresponding prudence, since they have a great deal
to lose. Even more than people who 'have nothing to lose
but their chains,' they value security. In recent years this
has become such a conspicuous characteristic of our present
situation that the phrase 'security capitalism' has come into
general use to describe the spirit of an economy in which
financial power is highly concentrated.

What 'security capitalism' tries to secure itself against is
overproduction, loss of markets, failure of consumer purchasing power to keep pace with industrial output: the very condition against which limited capitalism would secure the
whole community. As Sir William Beveridge has pointed
out in this connection, 'Many of the restrictive practices of
business in the way of parceling out markets, fixing minimum prices, making difficult the entry of new competitors,
are like the restrictive customs of trade unions, in being
measures of defense against deficiency of demand.'

From this Beveridge concludes that 'The justification for
these measures will be destroyed and the principal motive
to adopt them will be weakened under conditions of adequate demand.' This does not mean that the whole problem of power would be automatically solved by the socialization of demand. There are other motives to the acquisition and exercise of power. It does not even mean that
assurance of adequate total demand would 'make competi-

tion work' throughout the economy. Beveridge means just what he says: that the motive to monopoly would be weakened, and the effectiveness of competition correspondingly strengthened, by the correction of the discrepancy in the flow of income.

There are large areas of the economy in which competition works reasonably well. As we have already noted at some length, it does not work perfectly. Under the institutions of capitalism — that is, so long as money means power — the struggle for advantage which is the essence of competition inevitably subjects the economy to oversaving and underconsumption. But if this defect should be corrected, competition would work much better than it ever has, not only where it still exists, but also in large areas where it has been suppressed. This would be true of the entire (and considerable) area in which production has been curtailed, markets allocated, and prices fixed by agreements entered into to protect an industry against deficiency of total demand. It would also be true of the area (likewise considerable) in which monopolists have charged what the traffic would bear and produced accordingly for no reason save their command of the power to do so.

There are still other regions in which economists are generally agreed that competition will not work. This is true of industries like railways and public utilities in which very large overhead costs are combined with variable loads in such a way that under 'cutthroat' competition it pays a railroad, for example, to get business away from a competitor by cutting rates to the point at which they just cover the 'incremental cost' of moving that particular bit of freight. Since such competitive rates do not cover the cost of building and maintaining the railway, such an industry is bound to go bankrupt under competition.

For such industries there is no workable alternative to monopoly; and since industries of this kind are strongly 'affected with the public interest,' economists are generally agreed that such monopolies must be conducted in the public interest. Whether this means regulation or outright public ownership is still a highly controversial question. Federal regulation has proved far from satisfactory even in the classic case of the Interstate Commerce Commission, and state regulation even less so. But public ownership is 'socialism.' Moreover, it would still inherit a multitude of knotty problems. What should railway rates, for example, be under public ownership? Should they cover only 'incremental costs,' leaving the cost of building and maintaining the roads to be covered by taxation as we do in the case of highways? Or should freight charges cover the whole cost? Should they also be used for taxation purposes, as some municipalities use their city-owned power and light systems?

Limited capitalism would not work like magic to solve all these problems without further effort. But it would contribute to our further efforts. In the first place, it would give us time. At present, discussion of these problems is conducted in an atmosphere of critical tension and general alarm for the future of society as we know it. Rectification of the flow of income would resolve the crisis by which absolute capitalism is confronted. But more specifically, rectification of the flow of income would greatly clarify all the issues of competition and monopoly. Under limited capitalism it would no longer be necessary to make competition bear the full load of responsibility for making the whole economy work. It would be quite sufficient if competition made a given industry work. Furthermore, the failure of the economy to work either under competition or monopoly would no longer press government ownership upon us as the sole remaining alternative.

Rectification of the flow of income would make the economy work, and therefore we should be dependent neither upon competition nor upon government ownership for maintaining an adequate total flow of consumer purchasing power. Consequently, our choice of the appropriate form of organization for any given industry could and should be based solely on the peculiar character of that particular industry. In some cases, no doubt, we would choose government ownership. We have already done so long since in many cases. But in every case the decision would be made without fear that what it really meant was the general failure of competition and eventual general abandonment of private enterprise.

26

The End: Achievement

THE VALUES of industrial society are in a state of terrible
confusion. This confusion affects not only our judgment of
what is most worth while, but even our conception of what
we mean by worth.

Since these matters affect the whole of life, our confusion
with regard to them affects all our thinking. But it affects
our social thinking most directly, and in particular any proposal to modify the established order of things. Some ideal
or other is implied in every social policy, old or new. But
whereas long-established policies can at least claim to embody long-accepted ideals, any departure must justify itself
anew.

This contrast is especially clear in the field of economics.
As the phrase *laissez faire* implies, that is the tradition of
letting things be. Whatever the values of industrial society
may be, *laissez-faire* economics can claim to represent them;
whereas any sort of economic planning must be prepared to
have its ideals challenged. Partisans of economic planning
are extremely sensitive on this point. Indeed, many of them
despair of meeting such a challenge in the present confused

state of our thinking about values, and therefore declare that planning can be done only in a relatively small area of life and even there only on the basis of otherwise generally accepted ideals. But this is a sadly ineffectual gesture. After all, who is to say what is a generally accepted ideal? The planners? Champions of tradition gleefully reiterate this question, from which they are protected by the character of their tradition. It is the basis of their claim that all planners are pernicious meddlers and even would-be dictators.

Limited capitalism faces this dilemma. We have argued that the flow of income must be rectified if society is to make full use of its industrial potentialities. But we have still to meet the challenge, 'Why should society do so?' Is industrial efficiency the master-ideal of Western civilization?

To many people this would seem to be a singularly crass and unspiritual ideal. Hayek, for example, explicitly repudiates it, in a passage which many readers seem to have overlooked. John Chamberlain, who wrote the foreword to *The Road to Serfdom*, overlooked it. For he summarizes the message of the book in this sentence: ' . . . "full employment," "social security," and "freedom from want" cannot be had unless they come as by-products of a system that releases the free energies of individuals.' This implies that abolition of governmental 'interference' (which is what Hayek and Chamberlain mean by releasing the free energies of individuals) will bring about full employment and freedom from want. But Hayek makes no such claim. On the contrary, he says, 'It is essential that we should re-learn frankly to face the fact that freedom can be had only at a price and that as individuals we must be prepared to make severe material sacrifices to preserve our liberty.' In other words, the ideal is liberty, not full production; the achievement of liberty will not bring full production; and why should it?

There is an answer to this question. It necessarily goes beyond the problem of capitalism and even beyond the field of economics, as the value-problem itself does. But in spite of present confusions, it is nevertheless quite simple and easily intelligible.

We all agree that the values we all seek, individually and collectively, are those of human life and personality, the fuller realization of our potentialities as human beings, a greater measure of the creative achievements of the human spirit which in some sense or other make life worth while. The question is, What do these fine phrases mean?

For the overwhelming majority of mankind throughout the ages the answer to this question has been provided by revelation and authority, and, conversely, faith and obedience. But the development of reason destroys the intellectual sanction of authority and the validity of revelation, with the consequence that reason now finds itself confronted with the immemorial question.

The classical theory of the organization of the economic life of the community through the medium of price is a part of the effort we have made to answer that question. That theory sidesteps the question by referring the whole problem to the individual conscience. This procedure, of course, coincides closely with the whole 'Protestant' trend of modern times, as many scholars have exhibited at length. For 'conscience' the eighteenth-century philosophers who laid the foundations of political economy substituted 'moral sentiments.' In their view moral sentiments embodied the natural law by which they thought the universe was benignly ruled.

Political economy translated 'moral sentiments' into the

'wants' of which economic demand is the expression. Thus, price theory reposes a very great burden of significance upon wants. What the price system does, according to the phrase that is most widely current today, is to bring about 'the efficient use of resources.' But the efficiency to which this phrase refers is no mere matter of engineering skill, nor does it refer to any economist's notion of what had best be done. Its appeal is rather to the consciences of all members of the community as registered in their 'wants.'

But what are wants? In recent years orthodox economists have made frantic efforts to avoid this question. The economist, they have insisted, must regard wants as 'primary data.' That is, he must accept them without inquiring what they are. Everybody knows what wants are, they say, and anyhow the question what they are and what they mean is a philosophic question of no concern to practical economists.

Orthodox economists have had good reason for avoiding this question. For wants are significant only if they have the sanction of authority and the validity of revelation. The natural philosophers of the eighteenth century, who believed that the heavens reveal the glory of God, therefore gave wants the authority of 'natural law,' just as Protestantism claimed divine authority for the individual conscience. Twentieth-century science no longer makes such claims. But the only alternative seems to be utter relativism.

It is the unanimous conclusion of psychologists and sociologists today that all wants are shaped by social experience. All that we know of human nature points to this conclusion. Whatever the requirements of the physical organism may be, the things people want are the things they have been accustomed to have or to see other people have. Their only sanction is that of existing practice, established habits, and prevailing tradition.

But this 'absolute relativism,' as it might be called, is nevertheless highly unsatisfactory, as a great many students have long since realized. Indeed, it is the source of all our present confusion. One consequence of it is the cynicism which has come to be regarded as the hallmark of intellectual sophistication. Such cynicism is the climate of opinion in which reaction flourishes. If the master-function of the economy is to satisfy wants, and if wants must be taken for what they are, why change anything? But for that matter, if people want what has been dinned into them, why not din it into them that they are the *Herrenvolk* and make them want *Lebensraum*? Fascism is not the logically necessary consequence of moral relativism, but moral relativism is fertile soil in which weeds grow faster than anything else. And how shall we distinguish between weeds and crops if the best we can say for democracy is that it is what we are accustomed to?

This intellectual nihilism is responsible for one of the strangest features of contemporary life: the effort of some of our greatest intellectual leaders to flee from the present into the past in the hope of finding — in medieval civilization, of all places — a moral authority which industrialism lacks.

But none of these escape mechanisms will do. Medieval civilization provided plenty of authority, but its authority is utterly at variance with all the facts of modern life. Fascism provides plenty of certainty, but we refuse to follow our own logic in that direction. Most of us even decline to accept capitalism as being our irrevocable fate, since its existence proves that it is what we want.

There is only one way out of this confusion, and that is by continuing farther in the same direction. Strangely enough, all this uncertainty is a consequence of the certainty of science. It is from science that we learned how relative values are to time and place. But science establishes something more than the relativity of values. It establishes itself. The resolutely objective scrutiny of human behavior reveals, along with the relativity of wants and values to the fashions of time and place, the progressive certainty of science.

Furthermore, science obviously does not stand alone. Viewed in historical perspective the panorama of human experience does constitute an amazing achievement the reality of which nobody can deny. This achievement comprises all the tools and arts and materials of human living. Sophisticates often sneer at such things as bathtubs and airconditioning. Taken by themselves, such things are tawdry manifestations of the human spirit. But why should we take them by themselves? Nobody considers these things the pinnacle of modern achievement. And what is the pinnacle of medieval civilization? The Cathedral of Chartres? But that, too, is just a building — only a pile of stones — virtually a gadget.

The truth is that cathedrals and bathtubs do not exist alone. They exist together. All the arts and all the sciences, from the discovery of flint to the measurement of Betelgeuse, have two things in common. One is their interrelatedness. All arts and crafts and sciences — all knowledge and all skill — condition each other. An achievement at one point makes other achievements possible at other points, sometimes it seems at all points. One science or one art does not flourish at the expense of others. We do not increase the sum of human knowledge by neglecting the 'humbler' mechanical arts, nor do we cultivate the humbler arts at the expense of greater knowledge. Taking baths in airconditioned buildings does not inhibit the writing of poetry. After all, the bathtub is our principal rampart against the scourge of medieval epidemics.

The other common characteristic of all the arts and sciences is their progressive development. This is what the historical perspective most clearly reveals. Even if the last five centuries are left completely out of account, the span bounded by the Aurignacian caves and the Cathedral of Chartres still represents an amazing achievement. To say that one society wanted caves and the other wanted cathedrals is simply ridiculous. The inescapable fact is that human experience does manifest a developmental pattern of some sort. To close one's eyes to it is simply to go blind.

These are obdurate facts. But the relativity of fad and fancy is no less obdurate. How shall we reconcile them? How shall we reconcile the certainty of science with what science tells us about the variability of human nature?

Since science also is a manifestation of human nature, the answer is obvious. Human nature has (at least) two sides. One is that of fad and fancy; the other is that of art and science, knowledge, skill, and ingenuity. Some values are those of fad and fancy. These are relative, notwithstanding the fact that such fancies are often very extensive and deeply ingrained in the habits and attitudes of a community — so obsessive that men go out and die for them with a smile of self-consecration on their lips. But at the same time some values are real, certain, permanent, and progressive. These are the real achievements of mankind. The Parthenon was a great architectural achievement and what it has contributed to the building arts of later ages still lives and grows, notwithstanding the fact that the worship of Pallas Athena was miserable nonsense.

That achievement is the real life process of mankind, and that is what we invoke when we speak of full production. Full production means the continuation and enlargement of the life process of mankind. That is what gives substance and meaning to those eloquent but otherwise empty phrases in which we bespeak human life and personality, the fuller realization of our potentialities as human beings, a greater measure of the creative achievements of the human spirit, and so on indefinitely.

Full production means the sum of human achievement. To sacrifice such attainment in some measure for the sake of some 'higher' value is to trade reality for fancies. The reality of freedom is what we achieve and have achieved by the cumulative skill of hand and eye and brain. The only alternative to this reality is some miserable superstition, the dogma of some tradition-obsessed community (perhaps our own), some tyranny of fad and fancy.

We need have no hesitation in committing ourselves to the ideal of full production, conceived as the life process of mankind. No conception in the whole range of human thought is richer in meaning, of surer logical validity or scientific soundness. This is true notwithstanding the fact that economists as yet are quite generally unaware of it. In a sense economists have had the idea of full production forced upon them by the shocking spectacle of suspended production. Those who have accepted it (and many still have not) have done so empirically, without having explored its wider meaning and even without fully appreciating what its acceptance may entail. But whether they know it or not, they enjoy very considerable support in their new position from two directions.

One is that of the philosophers. Political economy was

created by philosophers, and economists have always pro-
fessed to defer to the larger philosophic truths. But the
founding fathers to whom economists therefore still defer
were eighteenth-century philosophers. Theirs was an eighteenth-century conception of human nature, pre-psycholog-
ical and even pre-Darwinian. Present-day economists often
declare that no trace of eighteenth-century moral philosophy
remains in modern economic theory, but they are sadly mis-
led. The study of economics is the study of one aspect of
human behavior. It necessarily presupposes some conception of human nature. For many years the commonest criticism of economic orthodoxy has been that it rests on an
obsolete conception of human nature. The fact that many
present-day economists fail to see that this is so only goes to
show how completely their traditions have cut them off
from present-day psychology and philosophy.

The conception of the meaning of value which gives significance to the idea of full production is no crackpot concoction of the present writer. It derives from what is generally recognized to be the most important development in
the field of philosophy in our time. This is commonly known
as 'instrumentalism.' Its chief exponent, John Dewey, is generally recognized, even by those who fail to grasp his meaning and therefore deplore his influence, as the most influential thinker of our time. The way of thinking of which he
is the most eminent exemplar has a host of practitioners
scattered through a wide variety of intellectual disciplines
and fields of inquiry. If it has affected economics less than
many other fields of study, that is largely because of the
natural persistence of eighteenth-century philosophy in a
discipline which was an offshoot of eighteenth-century philosophy; and if the present writer is an exception to this rule,

he is by no means the only one, and the fact is no particular credit to him, since he grew up in the atmosphere of instrumentalism. The important thing is that an economics which thinks in terms of full production has the support of present-day philosophy to a degree no less, certainly, than that which eighteenth-century philosophy gave to eighteenth-century economics.

It also enjoys a very considerable measure of support from the unreflective and (in the popular sense) instinctive attitude of a large part of the community. For in spite of the persistence of ancient dogma, the man in the street is singularly realistic. He sees the part that machine technology plays in modern life. He is therefore increasingly convinced of the importance of the physical aspect of what we still call 'capital,' and increasingly skeptical of financial considerations; and when the machines stop, his unreflective feeling is that realities have been sacrificed to fancies.

He is right; and as time goes on he will find out more and more fully just why he is right and just how right he is. For truth is great and will prevail. The moral confusion of our day is the counterpart of our social confusion. As we go forward, both will pass.

27

Facing Social Change

THE IDEA that deliberate planning must take the place of the planless growth of recent centuries has won if not general at least wide acceptance. Under such enlightened leadership as that of Mr. Eric Johnston even organizations of businessmen have come to accept if not to relish the larger rôle which government will inevitably play in these adjustments. But a considerable residue of apprehension still remains. A great many otherwise sane and reasonable people are still thrown into a panic bordering on hysteria by the ever-recurring question, What is it all leading to?

It is to this question that the present book has been addressed. The problems of economic planning lead in many directions. Some of these — a representative sample, it is hoped — have been indicated in the preceding chapters. But the object of these chapters has not been to unroll a blueprint of a planned economy. Our purpose has been at the same time more limited and more ambitious. All the difficulties of detail which the growing complexity of the industrial economy has forced on our attention have a common focus. Nobody can work out a complete blueprint of a

planned society. Nobody can possibly know in full detail
what is coming after capitalism. This is true, not only because more than one alternative is possible, but also and
even more pertinently because the subject is too large. But
this does not mean that the future is a complete blank.

We have learned a great deal from the sad experiences of
recent decades. Meantime we have also learned a great deal
through the advancement of science. After all, a century
has not yet passed since Darwin brought mankind within
the orbit of the natural sciences. It has been a busy century.
Obviously, we have much to learn — in a certain sense more
than ever before, since our awareness of the magnitude of
our ignorance is continually growing. But already we do
know a great deal about ourselves, about human behavior
and social structure, about our past and the vast perspective
of social development, knowledge with which no previous
generation has been equipped.

In particular we know a great deal about social change,
and that knowledge makes our worst fears utterly gratu-
itous. The worst fear is fear of the unknown. No dentistry
is absolutely painless, nor is any social change. But no den-
tal operation is so unendurable as to justify the paroxysms
of apprehension into which hysterical patients sometimes
work themselves, nor is any social change. It is true of social
change as it is of dentistry that the agony can be greatly reduced by foreknowledge and co-operation.

We have sometimes indulged in speculation concerning
the possibility that industrial society might destroy itself
utterly and disappear from the face of the earth. But this is
most unlikely. It may sound fatuous to say that history
reveals no previous instance of such a disappearance, since
history reveals no previous instance of industrial society.

But we can say with absolute certainty that we have explored every corner of the earth without finding any evidence whatever that any society of the order of magnitude of our own has ever disappeared. The lost Atlantis is only a myth. No continent ever sank into the ocean, and no great civilization — that is, one that would leave ruins comparable to those we know — has ever sunk into oblivion. Great ruins do exist in regions which are now remote from centers of population. But in every case they are known to be the work of civilizations which persisted elsewhere or were supplanted and in large part absorbed by other and greater civilizations, greater at least in the magnitude of the ruins which they left in turn. The fanatical Conquistadores who burned the Mayas' books may not have been gentler or more gracious than the 'heathen' they subdued, but they did have books of their own — even more than the Mayas. To imagine the complete disappearance of industrial society would call for greater genius than that of Mr. H. G. Wells. He has supposed it to have happened. But even he has been singularly vague as to how such a thing might come about.

It is doubtful if any major institution ever disappears. The growth of science and industrial technology has (for it is all one) subjected all the institutions of Western society to very great strain. One after another they have been undergoing major transformations. Two, the church and the family, have already emerged in greatly altered form. Does anyone doubt this? His doubt is evidence of our ability to adjust ourselves to changes which once occasioned the same dread with which our contemporaries contemplate the present change. For the church has been in large measure 'separated' from the state, and by virtue of this separation it is now quite a different institution from what it was. And the same is true of the family. Once the basic occupational unit of society, the family has come to have little more than a residential meaning; and even as a residential unit it has come to consist of little more than husband and wife and their growing children, if any. The elderly parents of husband and wife, and all their aunts, uncles, brothers and sisters, not to mention cousins and remoter relatives, and even their own grown children, all now reside elsewhere. The sum total of this change is very considerable. For many generations prophets and moralists viewing it in prospect cried: 'Woe! Woe!' Nevertheless, we have survived to wonder at the intensity of their alarm.

The major institutions which are now undergoing greatest change are the state and property. Indeed, both have already been altered far more substantially than most people are aware. The modern state, with its sovereignty over vast areas, in some cases extending virtually all the way around the earth, and over great masses of people, in some cases running to hundreds of millions, and with its responsibility for the operation of a prodigiously complicated social and economic mechanism, is as different from the principalities of feudal times as they were from savage tribes, perhaps even more so. Charlemagne or Genghis Khan would feel no more at home than Sitting Bull in present-day Washington or London or Moscow.

And the same is true of property. We have already noted the complex and varied assortment of functions which property performs and the changes which the assortment has undergone during the last half-dozen centuries and even during the last half-dozen decades. In the first instance property has been detached in large degree from lineage and hereditary rank and has become much more freely transferable than was formerly the case; and in recent decades, as we have already noted, a further dissociation of receipt of income from control and management has been going on. At the same time, each of these several functions has been undergoing modification, and it is only reasonable for us to expect further modification in the future. This does not mean that any one of them may be expected to disappear. None has altogether disappeared even in the Soviet Union. Transfer of authority for the determination of legal identity and parentage from the church to the Bureau of Vital Statistics has not yet led to the disappearance of the sacrament of baptism, and may never do so. It is at least no less likely that individual economic power both in the form of managerial control and in that of vested right to income will continue to prevail in some form or other.

The emphasis upon the accumulation of funds — indeed, the emphasis upon funds rather than upon the physical realities of production and consumption — which has been the distinguishing feature of Western civilization during the past few centuries will certainly be reduced. It is that feature of our civilization which is designated most definitely by the term 'capitalism.' In this sense it seems clear that capitalism will pass away, but only in this sense. The change need involve no sacrifice on anybody's part of luxury, or comfort, or freedom, or initiative, or indeed of any of the realities of our civilization. Only our fancies with regard to the divinity of capital would suffer attrition.

Nevertheless, we must not underestimate the importance of fancies. Although it is only this one recent, unique, and highly dubious feature of our economy which has justified the designation 'capitalism,' many people have come to associate this term with all that life holds in store for them.

That association is not unnatural. Many Englishmen once felt the same about their king. Such a sentiment is a kind of metonymy, the same kind that inspires lovers to identify all that life holds dear with the person of the loved one. As such it is only a figure of speech. The sentiments which inspire such extravagant expressions, however exalted they may seem, are never realistic. We all recognize that people who withdraw from life following the death of a loved one are emotionally sick. So are the people who feel that it were better that civilization should collapse utterly, and fading leave not a wrack behind, than that the present income pattern should be altered one iota — from whatever it may be at the moment of utterance, for of course it is continually changing.

Nevertheless, mental sickness is a fact that must be reckoned with. Realistic economists have been far too much inclined to disregard the sick fancies of their contemporaries. In this spirit Sir William Beveridge insists that his program 'by-passes the socialist-capitalist controversy.' For, he declares, 'it can be accepted by persons holding many different views on that controversy — by those who desire socialism at once, by those who oppose socialism at any time, and by those who are prepared to judge private enterprise and public enterprise on their merits in the light of experience.' In the same spirit an American economist recently advocated a similar program as the way of salvation for free private enterprise. So far as realities go, both are right. But both completely ignore the realm of fancies in which the outcome of the controversy may, after all, be finally determined. Both might well have taken a leaf from the experiences of an old heretic. In explaining why he was professionally ostracized for his espousal of underconsumptionism in 1889,

J. A. Hobson points out very simply that underconsumptionism, though it does no real harm to anybody, does challenge
the moral basis of capitalism.

For the essence of capitalism is that saving is an act of
grace. Such being the case, it is, as Hobson says, 'idle to pro-
test' that an argument against oversaving 'was not directed
against individual thrift, that it left open to any thrifty individual to spend as little as he chose of his income and to
save as much'; and it is no less idle to point out that what is
wrong with capitalism is 'a very simple fallacy, viz., the con-
tention that what anyone can do, all can do.' Capitalism
itself rests on the belief that saving is always a good thing
and that there can never be too much of a good thing. As
Hobson says, 'How could there be any limit to the amount
of useful saving when every item of saving went to increase
the capital structure and the fund for paying wages? Sound
economists could not fail to view with horror an argument
which sought to check the source of all industrial progress.'

That is why this book begins and closes on the ideational
note. More than by anything else, the outcome of the present crisis will be determined by the idea of capital — the
state of mind which makes all the difference between absolute capitalism and limited capitalism. Are we ready for
so momentous a change? Will the sentiments of the community respond to industrial realities? Such things take time.
When the British finally achieved limited monarchy in 1688,
the idea underlying this great change had been under discussion for more than half a century. Will the solution of
our present crisis wait so long?

It is indeed doubtful if we still have fifty years in which
to revise our sentiments. But it is also doubtful if we still
need so long. After all, a great deal of water has already

gone over the dam. The ideas we are considering are by no means new. Hobson's heresy can be found in our economic literature as far back as that literature goes, and more than fifty years have already elapsed since he forfeited his professional career by collaborating with Mummery in *The Physiology of Wealth*. Many otherwise 'sound' economists no longer view this heresy with the horror their predecessors felt. Something very like it has been espoused by Lord Keynes and Sir William Beveridge in England and in America by eminent professors in leading universities, past-presidents of the American Economic Association, and intimates of government departments.

The same interval has witnessed two global wars and the Great Depression (not to mention the one that brought forth Populism in the eighteen-nineties), the rise of the Soviet Union, and now the triumph of socialism in Great Britain. 'Full employment' has replaced 'the stewardship of wealth' as the order of the day.

The present order of society can be saved, and there is much to be said for saving it. But it can be saved only by the abandonment of capitalism as it is conceived by capitalists and their spokesmen, present and past. This should be possible. Otherwise why are we so much concerned about achieving full production? Such concern can only mean that we mistrust the basic theorem of absolute capitalism, that money always and necessarily provides employment. This mistrust is now shared by the capitalists themselves. Otherwise why should they feel any concern about the volume of employment? And why are they so greatly exercised over 'investment opportunities'? According to the gospel of capitalism there can be no such thing as unemployment or lack of investment opportunities. In spite of all the bluster about 'government interference' frightening off the sensitive and timid investor of 'venture capital' — that bold pioneer for whom risk-taking is the breath of life! — all this dismay over the drying-up of investment opportunities can mean only that capitalists themselves have lost faith in the creative potency of capital funds.

But this mistrust has to be recognized, admitted, and accepted as the basis of consistent action. We shall not make the present economy work by seeking full production through a strategy based on our doubt of the efficacy of capital accumulation and at the same time dulling the edge of the instruments of such a policy in deference to our continued veneration of capital accumulation.

If the veneration of capital funds should go, what would remain? As inheritors of the tradition of parliamentary democracy, we ought to be able to answer that question easily and simply. What remained after the disappearance of the divine right of kings? When the British settled this issue, they did not dispense with monarchy. It was unnecessary to do so. Once the principle of parliamentary democracy had been clearly asserted and firmly established, kings were no longer dangerous. It may be argued that they are also not particularly useful, as kings, and doubtless this is true. But at all events, Britain was saved the tremendous cost of total revolution. The Puritan Revolution had already given the country some notion of what that cost would be. It proved to be unnecessary, once the doctrine of divine right had been clearly and finally abandoned. What remained was, in form, a monarchy. But it was a limited monarchy.

If we were now to dispense with the divine right of capital, but without total revolution, the result would be a sort of limited capitalism. This would fail to satisfy total revolutionists and absolute capitalists, just as limited monarchy failed to satisfy dogmatic republicans and devout believers in the divinity of kings. But it would work, just as Britain's limited monarchy has worked, because it would immediately save us from the disaster to which we are doomed by absolute capitalism; and it would be susceptible to gradual progressive modification, just as British parliamentary democracy has been.

Limited capitalism can be made to work. But the limitation must be clear, definite, and final. We shall not achieve it by protestations of innocence. Capital must be purged clean of all odor of sanctity. The very idea of the supreme beneficence of funds must go. All the residue of traditional belief and sentimental fancy which now obstructs the rectification of the flow of income must be dispelled. Once that is done, all the rest will be simple and easy. Until that is accomplished, nothing conclusive can be done.

THE END

NOTES

MOST OF THE MATTERS touched upon in this book were discussed at greater length in an earlier book by the same writer: *The Theory of Economic Progress* (Chapel Hill, 1944). This is true in particular of basic concepts such as 'capital.' Consequently, it seems unnecessary to give detailed references to a book that bears so general and pervasive a relationship to the present one.

Chapter 1. The discrepancy between the 'industrial' and the 'pecuniary' aspects of capital, and of economic process generally, is developed most clearly and fully in the works of Thorstein Veblen. See especially *The Theory of Business Enterprise* (New York, 1904). For his most explicit treatment of the concept of capital see the pair of articles, 'On the Nature of Capital,' written in 1908 and reprinted in *The Place of Science in Modern Civilization and Other Essays* (New York, 1919). Karl Marx also made this distinction, as witness the chapter entitled 'Transformation of Money into Capital,' *Capital,* Book I, Part II, Chapter IV. But he placed greater emphasis on private ownership of 'the instruments of production,' and so treated as a struggle between classes what Veblen saw as a confusion of ideas. Virtually all orthodox economists now recognize the two senses in which the term 'capital' is used, and some have even warned their colleagues of the danger of confusing these two meanings. Notable instances of such a warning will be found in the article by Frank A. Fetter entitled 'Capital,' in the *Encyclopaedia of the Social Sciences,* and an article by Edwin Cannan entitled 'Capital and the Heritage of Improvement,' in *Economica,* New Series No. 4 (November, 1934).

Chapter 2. The quotation on early capitalist pressure politics is from *Early British Economics,* by Max Beer (London, 1938), page 72; that on the great transformation of the sixteenth century is from *Religion and the Rise of Capitalism,* by R. H. Tawney (New York and London, 1926), page 163. The instance of the textbook treatment of 'capital' is cited from *Principles of Economics,* by F. B. Garver and A. H. Hansen (Boston, first edition 1928), pages 153, 154. Similar instances can be found in nearly all the general or elementary textbooks.

Chapter 3. The classic account of the supposed 'spirit' of capitalism by Werner Sombart in *Der Moderne Kapitalismus* (Leipzig and Munich, 1902-1928) has never been available in English; but it has been widely discussed, most notably by Talcott Parsons in *The Structure of Social Action* (New York, 1937). See also the brief but keenly critical article by Abram L. Harris, 'Sombart and German (National) Socialism,' *Journal of Political Economy,* December, 1942. The classic account of the supposed dependence of capitalism upon Protestantism is by Max Weber in *Protestant Ethic and the Spirit of Capitalism* (London, 1930). For criticism of Weber see H. M. Robertson, *Aspects of the Rise of Economic Individualism* (Cambridge, England, 1933).

Chapter 4. The continuity of 'the industrial revolution of the eighteenth century' with industrial developments of essentially the same character which were going on long before that century is nowhere more clearly seen than in *The Rise of the British Coal Industry,* by John U. Nef (London, 1932). The idea of western Europe as a frontier of ancient civilization is broached by Henri Pirenne in his *Economic and Social History of Medieval Europe* (London, 1936). The discovery of a revolution in transport in the tenth century was the work of Richard Le Fèbvre des Noëttes. See also C. H. Haskins, *The Renaissance of the Twelfth Century* (Cambridge, Massachusetts, 1927). For a very fine account of the introduction of printing into Europe see Thomas F. Carter, *The Invention of Printing in China and Its Spread Westward* (New York, 1925). For the rôle of technology in social process see the classic *Instinct of Workmanship,* by Thorstein Veblen (New York, 1913). Veblen's idea has been very clearly presented in a recent book by Carl Dreher, *The Coming Showdown* (Boston, 1942), which opens with the sentence, 'Technology is permanent revolution.'

Chapter 5. For a classic discussion of the national (or social) dividend see A. C. Pigou, *Wealth and Welfare* (London, 1912). For the rôle of the community in the creation of the social dividend see again Veblen's articles 'On the Nature of Capital' in *The Place of Science in Modern Civilization* (New York, 1919).

Chapter 6. By far the clearest and most succinct account of the dilemma of saving which has appeared to date is to be found in a recent book by H. Gordon Hayes, *Spending, Saving, and Employment* (New York, 1945). This book is especially noteworthy for its amazingly clear and brief summaries of the work of Keynes, Hansen, Hobson, and other exponents of 'oversaving.'

Chapter 7. See *Spending, Saving, and Employment.* For an excellent example of 'pendulum' theory, see the article by Frank H. Knight, 'The Business Cycle, Interest, and Money: A Methodological Approach,' *Review of Economic Statistics,* May, 1941, in which the author likens the economy to 'a machine self-regulated by a governor' which 'always controls the regulated phenomenon — the speed of an engine, the temperature of a room, etc. — within some limits, between which it oscillates in a more or less regular or rhythmic cycle.' The clearest demonstration of the discrepancy in the flow of income is that of A. B. Adams in *The Trend of Business, 1922 to 1932* (New York, 1932). The classic study of the discrepancy between actual production and industrial capacity is that of the Brookings Institution, *America's Capacity to Produce* (Washington, 1934). For a very clear and brief account of the 'multiplier' see Sir William H. Beveridge, *Full Employment in a Free Society* (New York, 1945).

Chapter 8. The classic study of capitalistic 'expansion' is that of J. A. Hobson, *Imperialism* (London, 1902), reissued in 1938 with a chapter on the contemporary situation. See especially Chapter VI, 'The Economic Taproot of Imperialism.' Whatever their other shortcomings, the Marxists must be credited with a clear understanding of this aspect of capitalism. See especially V. I. Lenin, *Imperialism* (New York, 1929). See also the eloquent concluding chapter of J. M. Keynes (later Lord Keynes), *General Theory of Employment, Interest, and Money* (New York, 1936); Beveridge, *Full Employment in a Free Society;* and Hayes, *Spending, Saving, and Employment.* For what happens to exported capital see Max Winkler, *Foreign Bonds, an Autopsy* (Philadelphia, 1933).

Chapter 9. For the revolutionary implications of the loss of moral authority which capitalism has already undergone, see A. B. Adams, *Our Economic Revolution* (Norman, Oklahoma, 1933), and George Soule, *The Coming American Revolution* (New York, 1934). For a classic prediction, by an American of the old school, that capitalism was in for trouble, see Brooks Adams, *The Law of Civilization and Decay* (New York, 1895; edited by C. A. Beard, 1943). The same author's discussion of the relation of institutional inflexibility to revolution, in *The Theory of Social Revolutions* (New York, 1913), is also a classic. For an astute appraisal of the contemporary situation see Harold Laski, *Reflections on the Revolution of Our Time* (New York, 1943).

Chapter 10. The literature dealing with revision of the flow of income is now enormous. But in addition to the works already mentioned, *An Economic Program for American Democracy*, by seven Harvard and Tufts economists (New York, 1938), is noteworthy for its clarity and incisiveness. The figures on productive capacity in 1929 are those of the Brookings Institution, published in *America's Capacity to Produce.* See also Harold Loeb and associates, *The Chart of Plenty* (New York, 1935). Those who have forgotten the hysteria of the early twenties should reread Walter Lippmann and Charles Merz, *A Test of the News,* a supplement to *The New Republic* (August 4, 1920) in which the authors analyze the reporting of the Russian Revolution from March, 1917, to March, 1920, in the *New York Times.*

Chapter 11. '. . . While the incomes of the masses of the people were rising during this period, the incomes of those in the upper levels increased with greater rapidity.' The Brookings Institution, *America's Capacity to Consume* (Washington, 1934), page 126. '. . . The pattern of income distribution in our society is such that, whenever the national income expands, intended savings expand at a faster rate than the national income.' Beveridge, *Full Employment in a Free Society*, page 342. 'Every form of income received by the upper economic group tends to be enlarged when times are good. . . . To be sure, the wage-earner group normally gets more income during such a period, but this tends to be very moderate as compared with the increases enjoyed by the owner-manager-professional group.' Hayes, *Spending, Saving, and Employment*, page 40. See also Adams, *Trend of Business.*

Chapter 12. The quotations are from *Full Employment in a Free Society*, pages 19 and 21. The classic description of the unemployed as an 'industrial reserve army' is that of Karl Marx, *Capital*, Volume I, Chapter 25.

Chapter 13. For a brilliant analysis of the factors involved see the articles entitled 'Institution' by Walton H. Hamilton, and 'Property' by Hamilton and Irene Till, in the *Encyclopaedia of the Social Sciences*. For Veblen's analysis of the modification the institution of property has been undergoing see *The Theory of Business Enterprise;* and for an acute discussion of Veblen's insight see John R. Commons, *Institutional Economics* (New York, 1934). The same process is discussed in another setting by Adolph Berle and Gardner C. Means in *The Modern Corporation and Private Property* (New York, 1932). In this connection see also James Burnham, *The Managerial Revolution* (New York, 1941).

Chapter 14. For the best possible appeal to private enterprise see the fourth volume of the Brookings Institution series which began with *America's Capacity to Produce;* H. G. Moulton, *In-*

come and Economic Progress (Washington, 1935), and a later publication of the Institution by E. G. Nourse, *Price Making in a Democracy* (Washington, 1944); also Eric Johnston, *America Unlimited* (New York, 1944).

Chapter 15. The classic argument for lower interest rates as a means of achieving economic equilibrium is that of J. M. Keynes in *The General Theory of Employment, Interest, and Money,* in the concluding chapter of which the author calls for 'the euthanasia of the rentier.' The brilliant clarity with which Hayes manages to summarize this argument, and the cogency of his criticism of it, are among the chief merits of his *Spending, Saving, and Employment.*

Chapter 16. The rôle of public works in a program of economic stabilization has been discussed in virtually all works dealing either with public works or with economic stabilization. Of those already cited see especially *An Economic Program for American Democracy.* This subject is well handled in *Mobilizing for Abundance,* by Robert Nathan (New York, 1944).

Chapter 17. Since it is the scope of social security which gives it significance for economic stabilization, investigations in that direction are pertinent even when their sole concern is the need for the alleviation of want and misery. This is true, for example, of the survey by the Social Security Board, *Social Security in America* (Washington, 1937); the National Resources Planning Board's *National Resources Development Report for 1943* on 'Security, Work, and Relief Policies' (Washington, 1943); and Sir William Beveridge's *Report on Social Insurance and Allied Services* (London and New York, 1942). For discussions of the bearing of social security programs on economic stabilization see all the works previously cited, especially that by Beveridge, which was written as a sequel to the *Report.* For discussion of the dire effects of the 'Speenhamland system' see Karl Polanyi, *The Great Transformation* (New York, 1944). But see also the partial justification of Speenhamland by Gilbert Slater in *Poverty and the State* (London, 1930).

Chapter 18. For a very fine presentation of the principles of progressive income taxation see Henry Simons, *Personal Income Taxation* (Chicago, 1938). Note especially Simons's argument for the inclusion of inheritances in current income for taxation purposes. For the rôle of such taxation in a program of economic stabilization see the works previously mentioned, especially *An Economic Program for American Democracy* and *Mobilizing for Abundance;* also T. R. Amlie, *Lost: One Trillion Dollars,* a special supplement to the *Nation* (New York, November 27, 1943). For the 'debunking' of public debt see the splendid article by Alvin H. Hansen, 'The Federal Debt and the Future,' in *Harper's Magazine* (April, 1942); also Frank D. Graham, *Social Goals and Economic Institutions* (Princeton, 1942). The possibility of a continuous increase of public debt is discussed in *Full Employment in a Free Society,* especially in Appendix C, by Nicholas Kaldor, though Beveridge holds that 'there are good reasons for meeting state outlay, as far as is practicable, from current revenue raised by taxation' (page 148). For the clearest possible brief exposition of the feasibility of financing economic expansion with fiat money, see Hayes, *Spending, Saving, and Employment,* pages 210 ff., and note references to more extensive discussions.

Chapter 19. The passage quoted from J. M. Keynes will be found in the concluding chapter of *The General Theory.* The sentences quoted from A. H. Hansen occur on page 23 of *America's Rôle in the World Economy* (New York, 1945); that from Beveridge occurs in *Full Employment in a Free Society,* pages 233, 234, and was repeated in the preface to the American edition. For the export of unemployment in the earliest days of modern capitalism, see Eli Heckscher, *Mercantilism* (London, 1935), Volume II, pages 76, 114, 121, 122, and elsewhere.

Chapter 20. A very clear account of the process by which general business expansion is self-financed will be found in the third volume of the Brookings Institution series, the first and second of which (*America's Capacity to Produce and . . . Consume*) have already been mentioned: H. G. Moulton, *The Formation of Capital* (Washington, 1935).

Chapter 21. For a most thoughtful and eloquent discussion of 'the strategy of equality' see R. H. Tawney, *Equality* (New York, 1931). The classic account of 'conspicuous waste' is, of course, that of Thorstein Veblen, *The Theory of the Leisure Class* (New York, 1899), now available in the Modern Library. For a lively exposition of the importance of mass purchasing power ('The one luxury which the rich cannot afford is the poverty of the poor!') see Gilbert Seldes, *Your Money and Your Life* (New York, 1938).

Chapter 22. Veblen's dictum on the relation of business gains to disturbances will be found in *The Theory of Business Enterprise.* A thoughtful and temperate statement of the conventional view of pecuniary incentives will be found in Graham's *Social Goals and Economic Institutions.* See the concluding chapter of *The General Theory* for a brief statement of J. M. Keynes's doubt of the importance of the pecuniary incentive.

Chapter 23. For a very fine discussion of 'the conditions of economic freedom' see Tawney's *Equality.*

Chapter 24. See F. A. Hayek, *The Road to Serfdom* (Chicago, 1944); also Ludwig von Mises, *Omnipotent Government: The Rise of the Total State and Total War* (New Haven, 1944); also J. A. Schumpeter, *Capitalism, Socialism, and Democracy* (New York, 1942). For a reply to Hayek's challenge from a leading advocate of 'economic planning' see Barbara Wootton, *Freedom Under Planning* (Chapel Hill, 1945). For a brilliantly polemical criticism of Hayek's entire argument see Herman Finer, *The Road to Reaction* (Boston, 1945).

Chapter 25. For profound wisdom Tawney's discussion of 'the concentration of economic power' in *Equality* is unmatched. For the definition of the defect of capitalism in terms of 'the absence of essential institutions' see Columbia University Commission, *Economic Reconstruction* (New York, 1934), page 97. For the bearing of economic stabilization on monopoly see Beveridge,

Full Employment in a Free Society, pages 203 ff.; also pages 190 ff.

Chapter 26. The theory of value suggested in this chapter has been more fully discussed in *The Theory of Economic Progress.* See also 'An Addendum' to that book in *American Economic Review* (December, 1945). Dewey's definitive statement of his theory of value will be found in *The Theory of Valuation* (Chicago, 1939). See also the title essay of his *Influence of Darwinism on Philosophy* (New York, 1910); also Veblen's essay, 'Why is Economics Not an Evolutionary Science?' in *The Place of Science in Modern Civilization* (New York, 1919).

Chapter 27. The passage quoted from Hobson will be found in his *Confessions of an Economic Heretic* (London, 1938). See also his *Free Thought in the Social Sciences* (London, 1926). The passage quoted from Beveridge will be found in *Full Employment,* pages 191, 192. Advocacy of a full employment policy as a means of safeguarding free enterprise is that of Robert Nathan, in *Mobilizing for Abundance.*

Index